Advance praise for
DON'T DIE BROKE
HOW TO TURN YOUR RETIREMENT SAVINGS
INTO LASTING INCOME
by Margaret A. Malaspina

"People spend years thinking about retirement, planning for retirement, and saving for retirement—which I think is terrific. But they spend no time thinking about what they can and should do with the money they've put away in their retirement savings plans. The issues are complicated. Mistakes are costly. And there's no dress rehearsal. *DON'T DIE BROKE* **CAN HELP YOU CRACK THE CODE. THERE'S NOT ANOTHER BOOK LIKE IT.**"

PETER LYNCH
Vice Chairman, Fidelity Management & Research Company
and Author of *One Up on Wall Street*

"**IF YOU ARE APPROACHING RETIREMENT, PEGGY MALASPINA'S BOOK IS REQUIRED READING. *DON'T DIE BROKE* OFFERS A PRACTICAL, EASY-TO-UNDERSTAND BLUEPRINT FOR MAKING THE MOST OF ALL THOSE ASSETS YOU HAVE WORKED SO HARD TO BUILD DURING YOUR WORKING YEARS.** Malaspina tells you how to maximize income and minimize taxes, when and how to take distributions from your retirement plans, how to invest your money in this new phase of life, and more. *DON'T DIE BROKE* MAY WELL SAVE YOU THOUSANDS OF DOLLARS DURING YOUR RETIREMENT YEARS—THAT'S A RETURN ON INVESTMENT THAT'S HARD TO BEAT!**"

GINGER APPLEGARTH, CFP, CLU, ChFC
Author of *Wake Up and Smell the Money*

"Government lawyers have wrapped your retirement money in red tape. **THIS CONCISE, READABLE GUIDE WILL HELP YOU UNRAVEL IT.**"

> JOHN ROTHCHILD
> Co-author with Peter Lynch of *Beating the Street*
> And Former Columnist, *Time* and *Fortune* magazines

"THIS BOOK IS A SURVIVAL GUIDE FOR PEOPLE WHO WANT TO LIVE VERY WELL AND VERY SMART IN RETIREMENT."

> SHELDON JACOBS
> Editor and Publisher
> *No-Load Fund Investor*

"THIS EXCELLENT BOOK CAN KEEP YOU, YOUR CHILDREN, AND YOUR PARENTS ON THE ROAD TO ECONOMIC HEALTH FOR THE LONGER LIFETIMES AHEAD. Pass this around to the entire family. It is never too early or too late to plan and save."

> DALLAS SALISBURY
> President and CEO
> Employee Benefit Research Institute

"Margaret Malaspina's **LUCID AND THOROUGH EXPLANATION** of the process for turning retirement assets into income is a **VALUABLE PRIMER** for investors who want to be educated when they work with their financial advisers."

> BARBARA LEVIN
> Executive Director
> Forum for Investor Advice

Don't Die
BROKE

Also available from
BLOOMBERG PRESS

Investing in REITs:
Real Estate Investment Trusts
by Ralph L. Block

Staying Wealthy:
Strategies for Protecting Your Assets
by Brian H. Breuel

Investing with Your Values:
Making Money and Making a Difference
by Hal Brill, Jack A. Brill, and Cliff Feigenbaum

The Winning Portfolio:
Choosing Your 10 Best Mutual Funds
by Paul B. Farrell

Investing in Small-Cap Stocks
by Christopher Graja and Elizabeth Ungar, Ph.D.

The Inheritor's Handbook:
A Definitive Guide for Beneficiaries
by Dan Rottenberg

A Commonsense Guide to Your 401(k)
by Mary Rowland

The New Commonsense Guide to Mutual Funds
by Mary Rowland

Investing in IPOs: New Paths to Profit
with Initial Public Offerings
by Tom Taulli

BLOOMBERG PERSONAL BOOKSHELF

Don't Die BROKE

How to Turn Your Retirement Savings into Lasting Income

MARGARET A. MALASPINA

BLOOMBERG PRESS
PRINCETON

This publication contains the author's opinions and is designed to provide accurate and authoritative information. It is sold with the understanding that the author, publisher, and Bloomberg L.P. are not engaged in rendering legal, accounting, investment-planning, or other professional advice. The reader should seek the services of a qualified professional for such advice; the author, publisher, and Bloomberg L.P. cannot be held responsible for any loss incurred as a result of specific investments or planning decisions made by the reader.

First edition published 1999
1 3 5 7 9 10 8 6 4 2

Malaspina, Margaret A., 1944–
    Don't die broke: how to turn your retirement savings into lasting income / Margaret A. Malaspina.
        p. cm.
    Includes index.
    ISBN 1-57660-068-8 (alk. paper)
        1. Retirees—Finance, Personal. 2. Retirement income.
    3. Investments. 4. Finance, Personal. I. Title.
    HG179.M256   1999
    332.024'01—dc21   99-14869
                                                          CIP

Acquired and edited by Jacqueline R. Murphy

For Elizabeth and Peter Adam

CONTENTS

ACKNOWLEDGMENTS

THE WRITING PROCESS is anything but a solitary journey. The many individuals who traveled with me in the course of writing *Don't Die Broke* would fill a small island—and probably wish that's where they had been instead of on the phone, or over lunch, talking to me about creating retirement income.

Jared Kieling, editorial director at Bloomberg Press, inspired me to pursue this topic, and my editor, Jacqueline Murphy, provided both support and encouragement through the months of writing and research. I am grateful for the enthusiasm both have shown for this project along the way.

For guidance, information, war stories, and many good ideas, I am indebted to the many financial planning, tax, and retirement experts who are quoted in the pages that follow, but especially to Lou Beckerman, Andrea Bloch, Mary Cusick, John Doyle, Tom Hohl, Russell Miller, Steve Mitchell, Tom Peller, Norman Posner, and Eva Ribarits, who gave unstintingly of their time and expertise.

I could never have met my deadlines without the help of Monique Johnson and Mary Lou Marion, associates at Malaspina Communications, and especially Karen Perkuhn, who pitched in on research and fact-checking and listened patiently while I cursed technology for eating files and contaminating e-mail.

Special thanks to my colleague Mary Rowland for her encouragement, for sharing her professional insights, and for our continuing friendship.

Without the prodding of my daughter Elizabeth, this book would probably still exist as a handful of yellow sticky notes, otherwise known as my proposal. Both Elizabeth and her brother Peter came to understand, and to dread, those terrifying words, "Not now! I'm on deadline!" Thanks, kiddos. Thanks also to the women of IMM Investment Club, who were generous with their ideas and humor. And thanks to Mom, Dad, Carly, Paula, Doug, and Kate. You took the pressure off with your caring.

Finally, thanks to D, whose superior math skills bailed me out when it came time to crunch numbers and who made every day better by talking bridge to me when I felt like looking for one to jump from. Your lead!

INTRODUCTION

HEN I WAS seven, a well-heeled family friend presented me with a porcelain piggy bank as a special gift for winning a local spelling bee. At my parents' urging, I saved my pennies, nickels, and dimes—it was the 1950s!—thinking about how I would spend my savings. I have long since forgotten what it was that finally pushed me to tap my nest egg, but I do remember the ultimate comeuppance: I couldn't get at my money without, literally, breaking the bank. Of course, I could shake the pig and extract a few coins here and there. But I distinctly remember wanting to get at *all* of my money—and having to make a very difficult choice.

In some ways, today's retirement savings plans are a lot like my piggy bank. After years of discipline and sacrifice as you put money in, the last thing you figure is that it's going to be difficult to get your money out. However, the rules governing retirement plans—such as 401(k)s, 403(b)s, IRAs, Keoghs, SEPs, SIMPLE plans, as well as the lifetime pension plans offered by some employers—can make it a challenge. Because they are governed by a patchwork of tax laws that have been modified many times over the past two and a half decades and pension regulations that have never been finalized, they don't always make sense. Rules that apply to one type of plan often do not apply to others. Different rules apply to retirement savings accumulated twenty-five years ago than to money that you're putting away today. And it turns out that some of the choices you make can be costly while others are entirely irreversible.

Although I have written extensively about investments for more than fifteen years, like most financial writers I have spent most of my ink emphasizing the importance of saving enough for retirement and investing it wisely. Frankly, I never thought very much about taking the money out. I figured you would just, well, take it out and spend it when you needed it. Which is not to say that I didn't know that you couldn't take your money out too early, that you had to take it out at some point, and, of course, that you'd pay taxes on it when you did.

The complexities of withdrawing retirement money came across my radar screen about a year ago when my friend Fran Conti, who is also a financial writer, told me that she had decided to roll over her 401(k) money from a previous employer into an IRA. Her reason was simple: She wanted access to more investment options than she had had with her former employer's plan. (The amount in question was significant—several hundred thousand dollars.) What she didn't know was that the process would take more than three months, dozens of phone calls, and several visits to a local investor center.

But this is not merely a tale of poor customer service. It turns out that her retirement account included more than her 401(k) money. Some of it had been invested in a profit-sharing plan and some in the company thrift plan, a more common savings vehicle before 401(k)s became popular. Because she did not fully understand the implications of her rollover request—her employer's benefits office offered no guidance and neither did the investment company that received the rollover—the money that was invested in her thrift plan was returned to her. The reason? It didn't qualify for the rollover because it was so-called "after-tax" money. She had lost, forever, the ability to shelter future earnings from current taxes. With better information, she might have made a different decision and come out thousands of dollars ahead.

Fran's story made me curious about why so little had been written on the subject of taking money out of retirement plans. One obvious reason is that many of the most popular plans are less than twenty years old, and most of us, for whom they will represent the single largest retirement resource, are still some five to twenty years from retirement. I started talking to financial planners and to retirement specialists, each of whom added to my understanding of the complexities of this topic. All of them expressed concern about how little most people know about the key decisions they face concerning their retirement money.

Many had horror stories to tell. The following one convinced me that a book that could help people understand the hows, whats, and whys of taking money from their retirement plans was a real necessity. Janet Briaud, a Texas-based financial planner who specializes in clients who have worked for educational and other nonprofit institutions, tells the story of a man who came to her for advice a little too late. He had retired from a Texas school district with a nest egg of $900,000—$600,000 in his 403(b) plan, the nonprofit equivalent of a 401(k), and $300,000 in private investments.

On the day he retired, Briaud's client rolled his $600,000 retirement plan money into an annuity that promised to pay him an income of approximately $5,000 a month for life—more than enough to cover the budget he and his wife had calculated for their retirement. Little did he know that he had put himself, his wife, and his life savings at enormous risk. For starters, he had broken the first rule of taking money from your retirement savings: Tap your regular savings first. Especially when you're younger than 70½, that weirdly arbitrary yet magical age at which you come under the microscope of the IRS, it's important to keep your tax-deferred savings working as long as you can. Second, by choosing a "single-life annuity," Briaud's client had tempted fate. If he dies, his spouse is left with nothing. His children, the joint beneficiaries of his estate, inherit nothing. He spent a lifetime saving $600,000—and an ill-fated walk across the street could wipe him out.

An uncommon tale? Not so, according to Briaud. Most people find themselves making decisions about their retirement plan distributions with little guidance, and often with deadlines ticking down. Few people understand the consequences of their choices—or, indeed, what choices they have. Unfortunately, once Briaud's client had made his choice, there was no going back. Which is not to say that annuities are necessarily bad. But clearly Briaud's client was so taken by the monthly income chart he was shown that he failed to consider any other factors when he made his decision.

If you're reading this book because you're thinking about retirement, chances are you've spent most of your time focusing on how much income you will need and whether you have enough resources to generate it. For most American workers, that means adding together what you're entitled to from Social Security, your workplace, and your own individual retirement savings plans and personal investments. If you own your own home, you should also review your equity. The fewer outside resources you can count on, the more you should consider tapping your home equity as an income supplement.

Because retirement is receiving so much attention today, it's relatively easy to find good information on these basic issues. There are even some generally accepted guidelines to help you determine whether you're financially ready. For example, retirement experts say that:

◆ You'll need somewhere between 60 percent and 80 percent of your current income to support yourself in retirement.

◆ If you plan on retiring between the ages of 55 and 60, you should feel confident that you can generate income for another twenty to twenty-five years if you are male. Add another three to five years to those figures if you are female.

◆ If you want assurance that you will not outlive your retirement resources, you should limit your annual withdrawals to 4 to 8 percent of your retirement assets.

These guidelines are valuable, but trying to scope out your own retirement is a very personal exercise. For example, how much income you'll *really* need in retirement can vary widely: If retirement means scaling back, simplifying, and slowing down, you may be able to live on less than 60 percent of your current income. If you have more ambitious goals or if you're very sick, you may need to replace your current income dollar for dollar in retirement.

Then there's life expectancy: If you base your retirement income plan on the averages, you could end up short, especially if longevity runs in your family. It may make sense to add an extra five or ten years to your long-range plan to be on the safe side.

And the rate at which you take money out of your retirement plans? Four percent is a very conservative estimate. It assumes that you will increase the dollar amount you withdraw to keep up with inflation and preserves the value of your assets so that you have an estate to pass on to your heirs. However, the historical inflation rate it assumes may end up being high or low. And leaving an estate for your heirs may not be your goal. On the other hand, if the value of your savings takes a severe plunge at any point in time, even 4 percent may seem like too much.

What makes it hard to be very precise about pre-retirement planning is that there are so many variables: And because you're almost guaranteed to be responsible for generating more of your own retirement income than individuals in your parents' generation—whether it's from a 401(k) or a lump-sum distribution from your employer or some other combination—you will bear more risk, in general.

What's more, you don't know whether you'll live out your days in good health or spend some of your

HOW INVESTMENTS HAVE FARED

	1926–98	1990s
Large-Company Stocks	11.2%	16.6%
Small-Company Stocks	12.7%	16.5%
Long-Term Corporate Bonds	5.8%	10.2%
Long-Term Government Bonds	5.3%	10.7%
Intermediate-Term Government Bonds	5.3%	8.0%
U.S. Treasury Bills	3.8%	5.0%
Inflation	3.1%	3.1%

Used with permission. © 1998 Ibbotson Associates, Inc. All rights reserved. Certain portions of this work were derived from copyrighted works of Roger G. Ibbotson and Rex Sinquefield.

years in need of costly long-term care. You can't predict how costs will change over the course of your retirement years. If some or all of your retirement income is tied to the performance of your investments, the best you can do is estimate a return based on historical averages (see the accompanying table). The problem is that near-term results may vary widely from long-term averages. And no one can predict the near term.

But this book is not about figuring out whether you have enough money to retire—although it could change your mind on that score once you've read it—

or how much it will cost you to live in retirement. If you have made the decision to retire and marked the date on your calendar, it's time to think about the resources that you have accumulated. I don't believe it's necessary to become an expert on retirement plan distributions, but it is important to be informed. And it can be costly if you're not.

Whether you're retiring for good, leaving one retirement plan for another because you're changing jobs, or just thinking about taking money out of one of your plans, this book can help you understand all your options as well as the potential consequences of the choices you make. It is organized to address some of the general principles of taking money from your retirement plans and to explain some of the quirky terms that you will encounter along the way. It explains the pros and cons of each major retirement plan distribution option and relates them to the many different kinds of retirement plans, so that you can understand precisely how to get the most out of the plans you are part of. It offers guidance on how to create a retirement paycheck, regardless of how you decide to take charge of your retirement plan money. And it talks about what's different if you own or work for a small business, if you are a professional practitioner, or if you're self-employed.

Although many people fear that they won't have enough money to pay for a comfortable retirement, it's a fact of life that if there is money left over in your accounts, it becomes part of your estate. How you plan for that eventuality may be as important as any decision you make about your retirement money during your lifetime. That's why I've included a section on your retirement assets as part of your estate, as well as a discussion of issues to consider if you inherit retirement plan assets that are part of someone else's estate.

In the course of writing this book, I have spent a lot of time talking to experts and expanding my own knowledge of the process of turning savings into retirement income. Among the most important lessons I have learned is this: The more complicated your situation—i.e., the more it departs from the norms you'll find discussed in detail in these pages— the more important it is to seek professional advice from a qualified financial adviser. It doesn't make a difference whether you have a lot of money at stake or a little. In fact, many financial experts believe that the *less* you have, the more important it is to make sure the decisions you make today will give you the best chance to get the most out of your money in the years to come.

Speaking of experts: In the very last section of this book, you'll find guidance on what to look for if you need professional help. An investment professional can be an excellent next resource once you have mastered the basic issues that are taken up in this book. If I've done my job correctly, you will be armed with intelligent questions. And you will have taken a very important step toward achieving a comfortable retirement.

How Retirement

Income Has
CHANGED

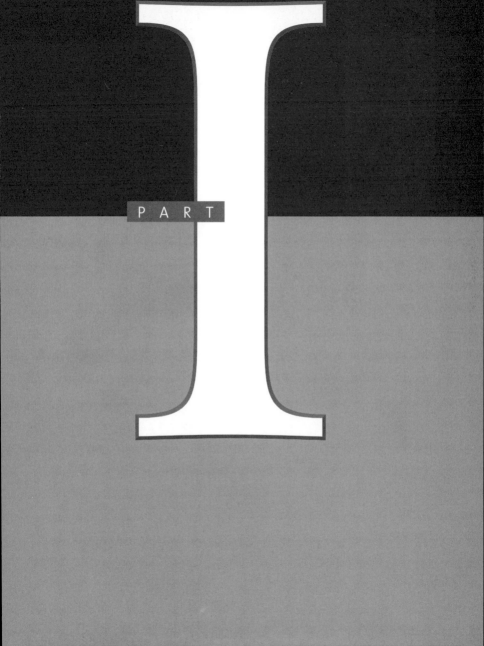

PART

I

CHAPTER

1

The Myth of Yesterday's BOUNTIFUL RETIREMENT

ID YOU GET a gold watch when you retired? I would be surprised if you did. Not that you didn't deserve one, after decades—or was it years?—of loyal service to your employer. The gold watch was always something of a myth. And it's not the only myth that has managed to work its way into the conventional wisdom about retirement.

FIVE MYTHS ABOUT RETIREMENT

Myth #1: In the past, most Americans worked all their lives for one employer.

If you changed jobs three to five times or more in the course of your working years, you may think that makes you different from the members of your parents' generation. There is a perception that in some not-so-distant past, people spent most or all of their working years with the same employer. However, statistics compiled by the Employee Benefit Research Institute

(EBRI) dispute that notion. According to Institute president Dallas Salisbury, only about 16 to 22 percent of the population ever spent a full career with one employer. "The world of work is becoming more like it has always been," says Salisbury, "high turnover." And because the number of jobs at small companies, where turnover is typically higher, has risen far faster than the number of jobs at large companies, Salisbury predicts that the level of job instability that has long been the norm for most Americans may soon be the norm for all but the tenured few.

Myth #2: Previous generations were covered by lifetime pensions.

"Everyone knows someone who fit that pattern," says Steve Mitchell, a retirement expert and senior vice president at Fidelity Investments. "Everyone has a parent, an uncle, a neighbor who retired from General Electric or General Motors." That's made it easy to extrapolate the notion that yesterday's retirees were taken care of better than you can expect to be. However, this one is full of holes. For starters, retirement itself is something of a last-half-of-the-twentieth-century notion. Social Security became effective in 1937. Employer-sponsored pension plans were scarce before the end of World War II. In the early 1960s, only 9 percent of Americans aged 65 or older received some level of income from private pension plans. By 1992, that figure had risen to 32 percent. But for many people, it is not enough to get by on: In 1992, private pensions accounted for only 10 percent of the total income received by people 65 or older. And because fewer than 5 percent of all plans that promise to pay a lifetime pension are indexed to inflation, they become even less valuable over time.

Myth #3: Most of today's retirees live a carefree existence of golf, travel, and time spent with the grandchildren.

Certainly some retired Americans achieve such a comfortable retirement. In fact, since the late 1960s, the elderly have seen their financial circumstances improve more than any other demographic group. The reasons? A 1998 Census Bureau report cites improvements in Social Security benefits, a booming real estate market, and more women in the labor force. However, only about a quarter of retirees responding to a 1997 EBRI survey reported a retirement that was not financially troubled. Many worry about not having enough money to cover medical expenses. Few were confident that they had done a good job in their financial preparations for retirement. Forty percent said that their actual standard of living in retirement or their ability to do the extra things they had hoped to do fell short of what they had expected when they retired. And although median household income for retired married couples is up over the past thirty years, it is still well below the figure for all households—$29, 210 versus $35,172.

Myth #4: American companies have abandoned their retirement plans.

Wrong again. Despite increasing regulatory complexity, higher administrative costs, and a reduction in marginal tax rates—which makes it less attractive for employers to kick in for retirement benefits—traditional lifetime pension plans are firmly entrenched in the public sector, in large companies, and even in some smaller companies that are covered by collective bargaining agreements. The bottom line is that the only places these *defined benefit plans* (so called because a predetermined formula defines how much pension income you'll collect and when you'll receive it) were ever firmly established is in large companies and large government organizations. Despite claims that these plans have been dumped by employers in favor of less costly plans—notably 401(k)s—few major employers have actually dropped their pension plans. The number of American workers covered by such plans has remained relatively stable since downsizing began in the 1980s. In fact, the number of defined-benefit plans has actually increased over the past decade at companies with 10,000 or more employees.

In the public sector, defined benefit plans continue to thrive. The one difference is that most of these plans are funded either in part or entirely by contributions made by workers on their own behalf. These contributions receive special tax treatment, just like contributions to 401(k) plans.

That said, it is also true that fewer companies today offer defined benefit plans. But the reasons are less sinister than you might think. Most of the companies that eliminated their defined benefit plans in the past decade were small, and many had been established primarily as tax shelters for owners and highly compensated employees. As rules and administrative requirements proliferated, maintaining defined benefit plans became more costly—and that made them a poor match with small companies. Yes, many of these were replaced by 401(k) plans, which require employees to contribute their own money and decide how to invest it. But the shift probably has as much or more to do with a changing workforce than with the demise of the paternalistic corporation.

Here's why: Small companies have never had much in the way of traditional retirement plans, and most of the new job growth over the past several decades has come from small companies. From 1987 to 1992, firms with fewer than 100 employees created 16.9 million new jobs, compared with 5.1 million jobs created by firms with more than 1,000 employees, and that trend continues. Second, as some of these smaller firms have grown into large companies, they have brought their "small-company" benefits mentality with them. "Microsoft and Starbucks didn't offer traditional lifetime pension benefits when they were startups. Now that they are big companies, they don't show any sign of changing," says EBRI's Salisbury. As these new companies supplant old-line large companies with their more traditional approach to retirement benefits, the proportion of the workforce that is covered by them is declining. But more than 40 million employees are still covered by defined benefit plans. No death knell yet.

Myth #5: Social Security will fail before the next generation retires.

Today Social Security accounts for approximately 40 percent of the total retirement income collected by Americans aged 65 or older. Yet nearly a quarter of working Americans believe they will receive nothing from Social Security by the time they retire. And no wonder. By the year 2019 it is projected that the nation's Social Security system will be paying out more in benefits than it is receiving in income. And somewhere near the middle of the first century of the new millennium, the Social Security Trust Fund is expected to run dry. However, that doesn't mean that Social Security itself would go broke. This is not an all-or-nothing game. Social Security reform has been the topic of serious debate during the past several administrations, and recently a presidential panel made recommendations on how to bail out the system through some combination of tax increases, reduced benefits, delayed eligibility, and privatization of some portion of the program through individual retirement accounts over which workers would have some investment control.

What's more, the notion that Social Security is headed for bankruptcy overstates the problem. You may not be able to count on it to support you, but that was never the program's intent. It is fair to say that the larger you expect your retirement resources to be and the younger you are, the smaller the share of your retirement income you should count on Social Security to represent. Yet Paul Yakoboski, a senior research associate at EBRI, estimates that if benefits were scaled back to 75 percent of today's level, the system would remain healthy with no further changes. Stay tuned.

SUBSTITUTING ONE
MYTHOLOGY FOR ANOTHER

EBRI PRESIDENT DALLAS SALISBURY points out that when it comes to thinking about where our retirement income will come from, Americans have substituted one mythology for another—and both represent extremes. "We have gone from a world that said everything was going to be OK, you don't have to save for retirement because your employer and Social Security will take care of you, to a world where we say that no one is going to have anything, that employers aren't doing anything, and that Social Security won't be there when you need it." Of course, neither image is accurate. And, as Salisbury points out, if you have to choose between the extremes, we're much better off today. Erring on the side of being better prepared than we need to be just can't be bad. "If your parents thought they were going to be OK in retirement, and they ended up not being able to put food on the table," says Salisbury, "that's a problem." However, if we've overblown the need to save for retirement today, what's the downside? That you might have bought a new car ten or twenty years ago instead of contributing to your 401(k)? You're better off economically—how can you complain about that?

CHAPTER

2

Why Tomorrow's Retirement Will Be Different—

AND WHAT THAT MEANS TO YOU

YTHS ASIDE, it is true that your retirement is likely to be very different from that of your parents or your grandparents. That's why the decisions you make about your retirement plan savings are so important. You're going where no one has been before.

For starters, you will probably spend more years in retirement than any previous generation. At the turn of the century, someone lucky enough to live to age 65 had already outlived his or her life expectancy by nearly twenty years. In fact, the average life expectancy for a male born in 1950 was 65.6 years. Now, if you make it to your 65th birthday you can expect to live another fifteen years if you are male and another nineteen years if you are female (see the accompanying table).

A longer life expectancy means that you need to plan your retirement income to cover the additional years and then some. Otherwise, you're accepting a 50-50 chance that you will outlive the averages.

AMERICANS ARE LIVING LONGER

HERE'S HOW MANY YEARS YOU CAN EXPECT TO LIVE . . .

IF YOU WERE BORN IN	IF YOU ARE MALE	IF YOU ARE FEMALE
1900	46.3	48.3
1920	53.6	54.6
1930	58.1	61.6
1940	60.6	65.2
1950	65.6	71.1
1960	66.6	73.1
1970	67.1	74.7
1980	70.0	77.4
1990	71.8	78.8

Source: U.S. Department of Health, 1996.

Some people think of retirement as a date, but for most Americans it has become a process. A recent University of North Texas study concludes that retirement today comprises three distinct stages, each characterized by its own pattern of expenditures and income needs. **EARLY-STAGE** retirees (ages 65 to 74), for example, are typically the most healthy and active. They are more likely to work at least part time and maintain an expenditure pattern that varies little from the one they had before retirement. It's not uncommon for early-stage retirees to conserve their retirement savings, to leave Individual Retirement Accounts (IRAs) and other retirement savings vehicles untouched until they are required to take money from them, and to postpone collecting Social Security or, at minimum, to manage earned income carefully in order to avoid losing out on Social Security benefits.

In **MIDSTAGE** (ages 75 to 84), it's more likely that retirement resources become truly fixed. And because of government-imposed minimum withdrawal requirements as well as actual need, many retirees begin to tap all their available assets to meet their income requirements during this stage of retirement.

In **LATE** retirement (ages 85 and beyond), spending patterns are likely to shift significantly away from travel and hobbies to cover higher health care and home-services costs, sometimes placing a strain on capital resources. The most important thing at this point is to have enough predictable income to help you live out your years in comfort.

Americans get a bad rap for having a low savings rate. But chances are that you have saved more for your retirement than your parents did. There is far more money at stake in private investments for retirement today than there was a generation ago. Retirement savings vehicles such as IRAs and 401(k) plans, which didn't exist a generation ago, account for more than $3 trillion today. (To put that figure into perspective, consider that the U.S. military budget is approximately $300 billion.)

What's more, today's retirement dollars are invested differently. More than 44 percent of all IRA assets and more than 32 percent of all 401(k) and 403(b) assets are invested in mutual funds today, compared with 29 percent and 11 percent, respectively, just five years ago. Not surprisingly, that shift has been accompanied by a move from fixed-income investments to stock and stock mutual fund investments with higher long-term return potential but significantly higher volatility. It has tracked one of the strongest bull markets for stocks in recorded history.

You have the opportunity to control more of your retirement resources than the members of your parents' generation. The fact that you are reading this book suggests that you have already taken advantage of some of the various retirement savings vehicles that have made it more attractive to save for retirement because of the tax advantages they offer. You've probably made some sacrifices to save. And you've shouldered the responsibility for deciding how to invest your money. Now that it's time to turn those savings into income, you are in charge of deciding when you want to take control of your money, how you want to invest it, whether you will pay taxes on it now or later, and who you will pass it on to when you're gone.

Chances are that you will rely on your personal savings to generate more of your retirement income than did those in your parents' generation. In a sense, that brings us full circle, back to pre–Social Security times when personal savings were all that most individuals had to retire on—if, indeed, they could afford to retire or lived long enough to retire. But you should be far better off than any previous generation if you've taken advantage of the many tax-advantaged retirement savings vehicles that have been created over the past several decades to encourage workers to save, and of the tax law changes that have continued to make existing retirement savings plans more flexible—and available to more participants. Today there are more than a dozen types of tax-advantaged plans that employers can choose to offer or in which individuals can invest on their own.

You will probably have more decisions to make about your retirement income than the members of any previous generation, partly because there's a good chance you have participated in several different types of plans over the course of your working life and partly because retirement legislation enacted twenty-five years ago helped workers qualify for retirement benefits with fewer years of service to any given employer.

In fact, the year 1974 is considered the beginning of modern retirement history in America. Here's why: In 1974 Congress passed the Employee Retirement Income Security Act (ERISA). ERISA's main purpose was to ensure that employers made good on the pension promises they had made to their employees. In doing so, it also increased the costs and complexity of defined benefit plans, which were the stock-in-trade for most large American corporations. Defined benefit plans are so named because they spell out a formula for determining how much an employee will receive in pension income, when payment will commence, and whether it will be paid over the employee's lifetime or extend to cover the lifetime of a spouse. In 1974, the onerous burden of ERISA's demands, in combination with a weak U.S. economy and rising inflation, opened the door for employers to look for alternatives. Some people think it was the death knell for the defined benefit plan. That's not true. However, ERISA did raise public awareness about retirement in general and, in a sense, launched the dialogue about retirement savings that continues today.

ERISA also created the Individual Retirement Account or **IRA.** Out of that grew a version known as the **SEP IRA**—a simpler, more flexible alternative to the **KEOGH PLAN,** which Congress had introduced in 1961 as a retirement plan for small businesses and the self-employed. In 1978, Congress added two more sections to the Internal Revenue Code— 401(k) and 457—which were interpreted to allow for the creation of plans that let employees make before-tax plan contributions. The first **401(k) PLAN** was offered by an employee benefits consulting firm, the Johnson Companies, in 1981. It was the brainchild of one of its own employees, Theodore Benna, who first saw its possibilities.

In 1996, many of the benefits of the 401(k) were repackaged for small companies in the form of the Savings Incentive Match Plan for Employees, better known as the **SIMPLE PLAN.** The newest retirement savings vehicle is the **ROTH IRA,** introduced in 1997 with a twist on the notion of tax savings: Account holders receive tax-free income down the road instead of an immediate tax benefit. One of the most compelling features of the Roth IRA is the possibility of converting previously accumulated traditional IRA assets to a Roth IRA, paying taxes on the earnings, and from then on receiving the income tax-free. Individuals with retirement plan assets outside an IRA can hopscotch to a Roth with an interim stop at a rollover IRA.

These are just some of the main types of retirement savings plans in which you may have participated during your working years. There are more. For example, if you work for a public corporation, you may participate in an **EMPLOYEE STOCK OWNERSHIP PLAN** or **ESOP**. Even employees in nonprofits can participate in a **PROFIT-SHARING PLAN** or a **MONEY-PURCHASE PLAN.** Your company may have a **HYBRID PLAN** that combines some of the best features of several different types of plans, such as a pension equity plan, a target benefit plan, a cash balance plan, a floor plan (a *floor plan?*), or a 414(k) plan. Most of these variations were designed to provide a higher level of benefits to employees who spend fewer than twenty-five years with a company. You may have participated in a **THRIFT PLAN,** many of which have been phased out and replaced with 401(k) plans. You may have had a **SALARY REDUCTION SIMPLIFIED EMPLOYEE PENSION PLAN** or **SARSEP** for your small business until the new SIMPLE plans came along last year. If you are an educator, a hospital worker, or an employee of a private foundation, you may participate in a **403(b) PLAN,** which you may know as a **TSA** or **TDA,** short for tax-sheltered or tax-deferred annuity. Or you may participate in one of the many public employee retirement system programs that cover federal, state, and local employees and have their own rules and eligibility requirements.

Which plans have you participated in? Before you take another step toward retirement, it's time to find out. And it's time to consider the decisions you will have to make to turn the money accumulated in these plans into income.

ZEROING IN ON

Your Retirement
RESOURCES

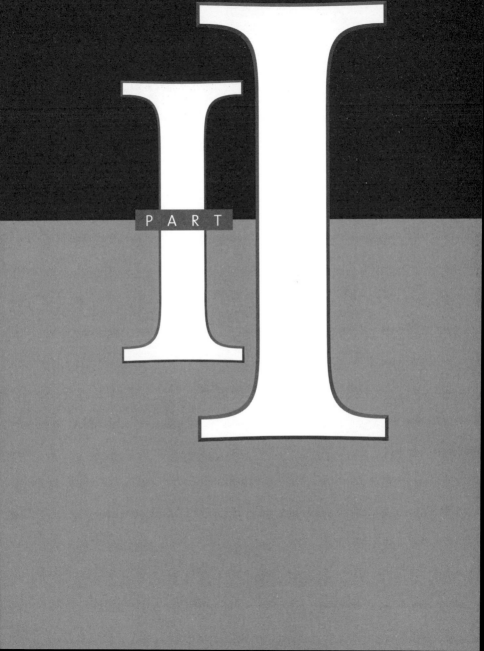

PART

I

CHAPTER

Where to Go,
What to Ask—
AND WHY

O YOU REMEMBER
your first job? It's not necessary to go back quite *that* far. However, if you are going to get all the retirement money you are entitled to, a look back over the majority of your working years is in order. The idea is to uncover any retirement plan assets that you may have left behind unknowingly, to identify all your major workplace retirement resources, and to organize your individual retirement savings so that you can think of them as one consolidated pool of assets that you will use to generate your retirement income. You will need a fairly firm estimate of the value of your pension benefits and personal savings and an idea of what, if any, choices you can or must make now. Finally, you'll want to have a clear picture of how you actually take charge of your money and whether there are issues of timing you should know about.

In the pages that follow, you'll find some ideas on

whom to talk to, what to ask—and why. The earlier you get started, the better. That's not usually a problem, since most people start planning for retirement a year or two before they actually make a move. However, not everyone is so lucky. Downsizing has presented many American workers with an earlier retirement than they would have planned on their own. Because it can take up to six months to put all your assets in order to create a retirement paycheck, don't put off these next steps until the last minute.

You'll notice that many of the chapters that follow have been laid out in spreads to make it easier to get at the information you want without having to wade through long sections that may or may not apply to you. Each spread targets a specific issue or question relating to your retirement money and covers it from start to finish.

DO A QUICK JOB HISTORY

USE YOUR COMMON SENSE in choosing a starting point, then list all relevant employers up to and including your current employer. Your goal is to come up with a rough accounting of the years you have contributed to Social Security, to check back on any money that might be coming to you from a previous employer, and to get a handle on any benefits, pension income, or both you may be entitled to receive from your current employer. This doesn't have to take a lot of work. Guess, don't agonize. If you discover money that you have overlooked, it will be worth the effort. By law, former employers have an obligation to try to locate you. However, if you have changed your address even once since your employment, that may be difficult. And they aren't required to exert any extraordinary effort, although in a sense it's in their best interest to find you, settle with you, and get you off their books.

How likely is it that you will discover a hidden retirement resource? "It happens all the time. You worked for a company ten years ago, stayed long enough to become vested in its defined benefit plan, which entitles you to a monthly payout at retirement, and you've forgotten about it," says Steve Mitchell, a retirement expert and senior vice president at Fidelity Investments.

But it is becoming less common as more and more employers offer departing workers the option of a lump-sum distribution, i.e., a payment of the estimated present value of the future benefits to which they would be entitled if they actually waited until retirement. That's certainly been the trend for the past five years. The reason? Says Employee Benefit Research Institute (EBRI) senior research associate Paul Yakoboski, "most companies find it more economical to get small balances off the books. It costs money to maintain them, and in today's market environment, the formula for computing the value of benefits is anything but onerous."

Back to your list. In one column, list anyone for whom you worked fewer than 1,000 hours in a year—roughly 20 hours a week, the general standard to qualify for pension benefits—and anyone for whom you worked less than three years. Unless you had a special agreement with an employer, even the most ambitious vesting schedule is unlikely to have given you access to company pension benefits with less tenure. However, these stints count toward Social Security and, at minimum, you'll want to be able to confirm your years of service when you check in on your Social Security benefits as part of your income planning process.

Besides, there are exceptions. If you were employed for even one year as a public school teacher and contributed to the state teachers pension plan—which is typically mandatory, because most educators are not covered by Social Security—you may have left retirement money in your account and forgotten about it. Today you can be required to take the money when you leave your employer if it amounts to less than $5,000. But that has not always been true.

In the second column, list all employers for whom you have logged more serious time. The process will work in your favor if you have retained records that indicate your vesting status at the time you left the company: your final benefits statement or—if you are really organized—a summary or highlights of your employer's benefits plan, which you may have in your files. Include your current employer in this list if you have been on the job long enough to earn benefits.

Then contact your employers. If you think you are entitled to benefits from a former employer, call. If you know you left money in an employer's plan instead of rolling it over into an Individual Retirement Account (IRA) or taking the money when you left, call.

Treat your current employer differently. If possible, arrange for a personal meeting with a benefits counselor. Bring your most recent annual benefits statement with you. If your employer has outsourced benefits management, a face-to-face meeting may not be an option. However, many employers offer seminars or question-and-answer sessions geared for workers who are ready to retire.

FIND OUT WHO'S IN CHARGE OF YOUR RETIREMENT PLAN— AND WHAT THEY CAN DO FOR YOU

IN A SMALL COMPANY, the person in charge of your retirement benefits might be the chief financial officer or the president of the company. Most larger companies have an in-house employee benefits department, typically part of the human resources area. But don't expect to get to the right person on the first phone call. And don't assume you're going to reach a real person—at least not to start with. I learned that lesson recently when I called to inquire about the current status of retirement benefits due me from an employer that I left nine years ago. I was given an 800 number that led me through a voice-response system. The good news is that the directions were simple. In exchange for my Social Security number and my birth date, I was offered information about three different accounts—my pension income plan, my profit-sharing plan, and my 401(k). I was particularly interested in the value of my pension income plan and how much it would be worth at retirement, some fifteen years or so down the road. The system quickly reported my projected monthly payout and offered to send me a printed statement. Current employees were offered the opportunity to model the value of future benefits based on years of service and projected salary increases.

I had the option of speaking with a representative when I reached the end of the line with the voice-response system. That's when I learned that the entire process I had just been through was the handiwork of the outsourcing company that had taken over the management of retirement plan benefits for my former employer. Ken McDonnell, a research associate at EBRI, says there are no hard data on this trend, which has been under way since the 1980s. However, Mike Jurs, a spokesperson for Hewitt Associates, a benefits consulting firm headquartered in Lincolnshire, Illinois , estimates that benefits management outsourcing has grown into a billion-dollar business, serving mostly large companies that believe they can cut or contain their costs and perhaps provide better service to employees by turning over the job of administering some or all of their benefits plans to benefits management experts.

The good news is that you may get more consistent advice from the outsourcing company. Besides being one of the largest and most established benefits consulting firms, Hewitt Associates is also the largest benefits management outsourcing company. It's fair to say that they probably know more about benefits than a steel or auto company would ever want to know. The only problem is that if you are dissatisfied with the information you receive or the way your requests are handled, it can be difficult to find someone who will intercede on your behalf. When I put some challenging questions to the service representative with whom I spoke regarding my former employer's plan, I got answers that didn't jibe with my own personal information. At first, the representative dug in her heels, because she was looking at data on a computer screen and didn't see any reason to challenge it. Then she offered to let me speak to a supervisor. When the supervisor couldn't answer my questions either, it took another two days for someone to call me back with a satisfactory explanation.

No matter who is in charge of your retirement benefits, you should be able to find out the answers to some key questions. First of all, you want to know what kind of plan you're part of—there are many more types than you might imagine. If any of your plans are defined benefit plans, you want to know the following:

◆ The projected value of your benefit at retirement.
◆ How the value was calculated.
◆ What distribution options you're entitled to.
◆ What you have to do to execute the option you choose.
◆ How much time the process should take.

There may be income and estate tax implications to your choices. Be sure to ask for a clear explanation, but don't base any final decisions on information you receive over the phone from a service representative.

FIND OUT WHAT TYPE
OF PLAN YOU HAVE

WHY DOES IT MATTER? After all, you're just about history when it comes to your working years. However, if you are going to get the most out of your retirement income, you need to understand what you're entitled to and any choices you can or must make. Trust me. This is complicated stuff, and the extra couple of minutes it will take to get the name of the plan and a few of its most important features into your head should be worth it.

Retirement benefits experts divide plan types into two categories according to two different sets of criteria: tax and legal status, and type of benefit paid. For example, there are **QUALIFIED PLANS** and **NONQUALIFIED PLANS,** so called to distinguish plans that meet the rigorous criteria of Section 401 of the Internal Revenue Code from those that don't. It is important to know whether you are part of a qualified plan or a nonqualified plan because this may affect decisions you make about your assets. Many people discover that they participate in both types of plans. Here are some of the main points on which they differ:

Qualified plans offer valuable tax breaks to employers and employees. However, into the bargain, a qualified plan has to operate under a special set of rules that govern every detailed aspect of the plan, from the amount of money you and/or your employer can put in to a complex formula for testing to make sure the plan doesn't offer a better deal to executives and other highly paid employees.

Generally speaking, qualified plans require more administration on the part of employers and offer more protection, in terms of both the custodial oversight of your assets and the actual protection against litigious claims by outsiders.

Nonqualified plans aren't necessarily bad. Many companies use nonqualified plans to defer income for top executives above the limits imposed on qualified plans. Many educators and nonprofit workers are covered by 403(b) plans, which are nonqualified plans that have been around since the 1950s, long before Section 401 of the tax code (which governs the operation of qualified plans) was written.

Experts who focus on the benefits side of a plan are more interested in whether a retirement plan is a **DEFINED BENEFIT PLAN** or a **DEFINED CONTRIBUTION PLAN**. Many employers offer both types of plans. A defined benefit plan promises to pay a specific benefit at a certain age, typically an annuity for life and sometimes extending though the lifetime of a spouse. The focus of a defined benefit plan is on what goes out of the plan: the benefit. With a defined contribution plan, the focus is on how much money you can put in each year—the contribution—and how much, if any, your employer has committed to contribute. One defines what goes out, the other defines what can—and, sometimes, must—go in.

In a defined benefit plan, your employer is responsible for making sure the overall plan is adequately funded to provide the benefit it defines at the time it becomes payable. With a defined contribution plan, your money goes into an individual account with your name on it, but there's no guarantee how much your account will be worth.

That's the big picture. Although there is a very clear line separating qualified from nonqualified plans, there are plans that borrow some of the best features of defined benefit and defined contribution plans and combine them into hybrid or nontraditional plans.

How can you find out what type of plan you have? For starters, ask the person in charge of benefits. You want to know

◆ Whether a plan is qualified or nonqualified.

◆ If it is a defined benefit or a defined contribution plan. Then ask for a summary of your employer's plan document. In addition to verifying the type of plan you have, it should outline other important features about the plan.

ASK FOR A SUMMARY OF YOUR EMPLOYER'S PLAN DOCUMENT

THE DETAILS OF ANY employer-sponsored qualified retirement benefit plan are spelled out in a plan document—a highly technical piece of legal writing. In fact, if you are participating in a qualified plan (i.e., a plan that meets specifications set down in Section 401 of the Internal Revenue Code) and are eligible for favorable tax treatment, your employer is required to provide you with a summary of the plan document that spells out essential information in plain English. Even some 403(b) plans have plan documents, although they are not qualified plans. But many do not. Reading a plan document or even a summary is not what most people think of as a good time, but it is the best way to get at some of the essential information in your plan. And it can be particularly helpful when you're planning to take money out of your plan.

There's basic name, place, and date information that may come in handy if this is a previous employer's plan. It's the sort of official record you'll want to keep on hand for future reference, with the understanding that information changes. Plans are required to update their documents regularly.

You can find out the plan's vesting requirements, which may help you settle any differences you may have when you speak with a former employer. Your lead is much stronger when it's clear that you've done some homework.

Likewise, your employer's terms of eligibility may be important if there is any dispute about an unusual situation such as transferring among a company's subsidiaries or rejoining the company after working elsewhere for a number of years.

It's important to note the plan's statements on beneficiaries. It spells out the benefits it will pay to your beneficiaries. In fact, if you don't name a beneficiary, the plan document may determine who your beneficiary will be. A

scary thought. A section on spousal consent requirements is included in all plan documents where consent is
required for you to make certain choices, such as elect a
single-life annuity or a direct rollover of retirement plan
assets to an IRA.

Distribution methods are explained in the plan document.
This is particularly important for participants in small
plans, which may make you wait to receive your distribution until the plan is valued at the end of its **FISCAL YEAR**—
another characteristic that is explained in the plan document. Your plan document also spells out exactly how your
employer will distribute benefits to you, as a participant, to
a former spouse who has been named in a qualified domestic relations order, as well as to your beneficiaries after
you've gone. That's why it's a good idea to keep your plan
document in with other records concerning your estate. If
you die before you collect a benefit from your retirement
plan, your spouse will have the ammunition he or she
needs to ensure that payments and settlements have been
fair and accurate.

Benefits valuation methods are explained in the plan document. As plans move toward a standard mortality table
and the adoption of a standard interest rate formula (see
page 51), that will become less significant. But for now,
it's a key piece of information to help you understand
how your benefits are determined—and to double check
their accuracy.

**If your retirement plan offers more than one option for
receiving payments,** these are spelled out in the plan document. The section on direct rollovers typically contains
information on how your plan handles this common form
of distribution. It offers some clues as to how you can
manage the process and what steps you can expect to have
to follow.

UNDERSTAND HOW YOUR RETIREMENT
BENEFITS ARE CALCULATED

WITH EVERYTHING ELSE you have to put into place for
your retirement, it's easy enough to take your employer's
word for the value of your pension benefit. However, it's
important to ask for a precise explanation of the formula
used for determining your benefits and the figures that
back it up. Of course, the value of your 401(k) or any
other defined contribution plan will be determined by the
success of your investment strategy and the performance
of the financial markets. However, it's essential to find out
when your plan is valued for retirement purposes—and
whether you have any options. You could get lucky, as did
scores of American Airlines pilots who discovered they had
the option of locking in the value of their company stock
at the market high in July 1998, thereby avoiding the late-
summer stock market debacle that took the Dow Jones
Industrial Average down more than 15 percent. In fact,
enough pilots opted for early retirement—and a higher
retirement account value—that the airline was put in a
scheduling bind.

These clauses were more common before the market
crash of 1987. Lisa Alkon, an attorney in the Boston office
of William M. Mercer, Inc., says that pilots in general enjoy
certain retirement privileges that are not widely available
to other employees—a gesture toward the extra hazards
of their profession. However, it could make a significant
difference to know when the value of your account is set—
and to keep it in mind as you count down to retirement.

The value of your individual pension benefits payable
from a defined benefit plan is determined by a formula,
and formulas differ from plan to plan. Generally speaking,
the benefits may be tied to your compensation, the number of years you've worked, or some combination of the
two. Your employer may pay you a flat dollar amount for
each year of service. Or it may be a percentage of your average compensation during your working years multiplied by
your years of service. Or perhaps a percentage of your high-

est compensation or your final three to five years' compensation. The percentage per year of service dictated by your plan's formula may be as low as 1 percent or up to 2.5 percent or more. The average is about 1.45 percent, slightly higher for professional and technical employees.

Here's how a typical formula works: If you are retiring and you have worked for the same company for 30 years, you now earn $60,000, and your employer's plan uses a formula that awards you 1.5 percent of your highest annual salary (in this example, the salary you're currently earning) for each year of service, your retirement income would be $27,000 per year ($60,000 ¥ 0.015 ¥ 30). The most common formula looks at an average over the past five years or the highest consecutive five years. On that basis, your payout might be slightly lower. The plan can also be designed to reward loyal workers more generously by weighting either the percentage or the definition of earnings in favor of those who have worked longer, earned higher salaries, are older—or some combination of the three.

Keep in mind that the monthly or annual benefit that the formula indicates may not ever change. According to the Employee Benefit Research Institute, nearly 40 percent of government-sponsored defined benefit plans offer cost-of-living adjustments over a retiree's lifetime. However, only 4 percent of defined benefit plans in the private sector build an inflation factor into their payout. That's particularly bad news for employees who leave defined benefit plan assets behind with decades to go before retirement. For example, my monthly benefit from my previous employer's plan was $300 when I left in 1991, payable beginning at age 65. Today that figure is still $300—and it isn't going to change.

However, it is worth considering the value of your benefits before you make the final retirement decision. If, for example, the formula your employer uses places a greater value on extended length of service (i.e., you earn additional points for each year of service beyond a certain point), you may be able to boost your retirement income significantly by staying several more years.

INQUIRE ABOUT YOUR DEFINED
BENEFIT PLAN DISTRIBUTION OPTIONS

DISTRIBUTION IS SUCH A technical-sounding word. But that's what it's called when money is paid out of your plan to you. The retirement pros needed a general word that includes the various forms in which you can take control of your money.

Chances are you will have at least two options for taking your benefit from your employer's pension plan. You're likely to receive the highest absolute dollar figure by choosing a monthly benefit that starts when you retire and continues until you die. Employers refer to this as a **SINGLE-LIFE ANNUITY.** If you're married and you have been the major income provider throughout your years together, this could work out poorly for your spouse. In fact, by law you're required to take your spouse into consideration when you choose a retirement payout option from a defined benefit plan. (No such restriction applies to participants in certain nonqualified plans.) And unless your spouse waives his or her rights, you are required to choose a **JOINT AND SURVIVOR ANNUITY** that would continue to pay your spouse after you die. The rules are very clear: The federal government wants to make sure that your spouse has the opportunity to stake his or her claim to a portion of your retirement income. It's also a way of underscoring the risks that you accept when you choose a single-life annuity.

The tradeoff is a slightly lower monthly benefit for you and typically some percentage—say 75 or 50 percent—for your spouse. Of course, if your spouse dies first, you might feel as if you really lost out with that option. Some joint and survivor options promise to increase your benefit if your spouse dies within a specific period of time—an insurance policy, of sorts, against such a misfortune. Some options even guarantee a certain level of benefits for a set period of time—ten or twenty years, for example—to insure against an untimely death. But if you divorce after you begin taking your retirement income, there's no way to cut off your former spouse (see the accompanying table).

The joint and survivor option was created as a gesture toward married couples, but employers will also let you name someone other than your spouse to receive survivor benefits. Why would you want to? If you're single and responsible for an aging parent, you can ensure continued financial security without giving up much in terms of the value of your payout, because you've chosen an older joint annuitant.

Today more than one-third of all defined benefit plans will also let you take a lump-sum distribution of your benefits. Here's what that means: Say you are retiring at age 65 and, based on the formula set forth in your plan, you're entitled to an annual single-life benefit of $30,000. Or you have the option of taking a sum of money that would be expected to generate $30,000 a year over your expected life span.

In order to figure what that amount would be, your employer must use approved actuarial tables and choose an appropriate interest rate—both key players in this exercise. Employers used to have more flexibility in their choices, but 1994 legislation requires employers to use a 1983 unisex mortality table and the annualized interest rate on thirty-year Treasury securities to calculate the value of a lump-sum distribution. However, because of the way the rule was written, your employer may not have had to comply until the year 2000.

So what is your annual $30,000 benefit worth today? A little more than $385,000. A lot of money—potentially, an immediate tax burden—and a lot of responsibility if you choose this option. Remember, if you're married, you can't take a lump-sum distribution without the approval of your spouse.

INQUIRE ABOUT YOUR DEFINED CONTRIBUTION PLAN DISTRIBUTION OPTIONS

COMPARED WITH A DEFINED benefit plan, there are more unknowns—and more variables—associated with a defined contribution plan. Forget formulas. Whether it is a 401(k), a profit-sharing plan, or an employee stock ownership plan (ESOP), you will have to take charge of your savings once you retire.

Generally speaking, you can do three things with the money you've accumulated in your defined contribution plans when you retire (or leave your employer for another job): You can take it, you can leave it where it is, or you can move it into another tax-advantaged plan to avoid paying taxes until you need it. If you have less than $5,000 in your account, your employer can require you to take it or move it.

Deciding which one of these three strategies makes the most sense for you is the subject of greater discussion in Chapters 4 and 5. However, when you are in the information-gathering stage, it's important to verify your options—and some of the purely mechanical aspects of your decision.

If you decide to leave your money in your employer's plan, will you pay for it? At some companies, employees who leave balances in their 401(k) plans are charged an annual account fee to cover the cost of providing service and mailing your quarterly statements. It may be modest—at Polaroid, former employees pay the same $15 annual fee that they paid as active employees—and it's spelled out in information passed out to departing employees. It's also easy to forget about because it is deducted before performance is calculated.

Will your former employer restrict your access to your money? Many companies limit the number of times a former employee can reallocate assets to three or four times a year. And some plans offer a more limited list of investment options to former employees.

If you decide to move your money into another tax-advantaged investment such as a rollover or conduit IRA or a qualified rollover annuity, verify that this option is available to you and be sure you understand the tax and legal status of your various accounts. For example, do you have both *before-* and *after-tax* money? Do you have money in nonqualified as well as qualified plans? You will need an accounting of the different amounts. Why? Because, by law, you cannot combine money on which you've already paid tax—for instance, money you've saved in a company thrift plan—and money on which taxes have been deferred. Most companies have an all-or-nothing policy: You can't carve up your savings plans, moving some and leaving others to maximize your tax situation.

Most important to you while you are in the information-gathering stage, what action do you have to take to roll your money over? How long will it take? What forms do you have to fill out? Typically, the institution to which you are rolling your money over will help you with the paperwork, but you'll have to get the process started. And, ultimately you're the one who loses if something goes wrong. It's best to understand the process and who is responsible for what and when.

If you decide to withdraw your savings, either because your account is worth less than $5,000 or because you have plans for the money, you should find out how long the process should take and whether you have any options for transferring the funds electronically to a bank, brokerage, or asset management account so that you don't have to walk around with a substantial check in your hands.

If you're employed by a small company, don't be surprised if it takes longer to get to your money. According to Lou Beckerman with Northeast Planning Services, Inc., a Massachusetts benefits administration firm, a departing employee may have to wait until the end of the plan's fiscal year or until there has been a one-year break in service. However, someone who is retiring—as opposed to changing jobs—often has more flexible options.

ORGANIZE YOUR INDIVIDUAL
RETIREMENT SAVINGS PLANS

IN ADDITION TO PLANS associated with your workplace, you may have accumulated tax-advantaged savings in an annuity or an IRA. You may have rolled over money from a previous employer to a rollover IRA. You may be self-employed or a professional practitioner with retirement savings in a SEP or a Keogh Plan. If you're in the vanguard, you may have already taken advantage of the new Roth IRA or converted assets from traditional IRAs into a Roth IRA. Exact figures are hard to come by, but the mutual fund industry estimates that about 35 percent of all Americans have contributed to individual retirement savings plans, either as a substitute for an employer's plan— because they don't have access to one—or in addition to an employer's plan.

You'll need some of the same types of information that you gathered about your employer-sponsored retirement benefit plans. You won't have a plan document to consult, but for each of these types of accounts you should have a custodial agreement, says Tom Peller, a Boston attorney who specializes in retirement plan issues. If you don't have a copy in your files, call the company where your assets are invested and ask for one. It will contain valuable information about such things as your beneficiaries, which you may want to review in the context of planning your estate.

If your accounts are spread across different financial institutions, gather your records, review your balances, and make sure you have current customer service numbers for all your financial providers. Unless someone manages these assets for you, the person who will decide how they will fit into your retirement income plan is . . . you.

Here's what you want to know about these accounts:
First, you want to understand what services you can expect from the financial institution(s) that holds them. Will they help you set up a withdrawal plan if you want to turn your assets into a retirement paycheck that is actuarially consis-

tent with your life expectancy? Will your financial provider offer any incentives to reinvest money you've been required to take from your accounts in the form of **REQUIRED MINIMUM DISTRIBUTIONS,** such as waiving load fees? And will they calculate your required minimum distributions for you? That's the amount the IRS will require you to withdraw from your tax-advantaged accounts each year once you reach age 70½. It may be years down the road, but it's worth thinking about now. The calculations can be complicated. It's nice to know that you can rely on someone else to do them.

Second, consider whether you might be better off consolidating various accounts in one place. If you are dealing with a bank, a brokerage house, and several mutual fund companies, it may become time-consuming to calculate required minimum distributions for various accounts—or even just to deal with the paperwork. But it's a good idea to postpone the implementation of a consolidation plan until you have settled on your strategy for turning your assets into income and a tactical plan for creating a retirement paycheck.

It's not too early to think about record keeping, especially if you have a variety of retirement resources. I spoke with financial advisers to get a sense of what works and what doesn't. Here's what I learned: File folders are great temporary holding places for receipts and odd-sized pieces of paper, but they aren't very efficient. Pick up some three-ringed binders at the local office supply store. Get the kind that has pockets on the inside cover. That's where you can put odd-sized, loose papers such as bank receipts or mutual fund transaction confirmations. Set up a binder for your official documents and statements relating to your employers' plans and a separate binder for your individual plans. Keep a section for each institution and one for each separate account.

TALLY UP YOUR PERSONAL SAVINGS

THEY MAY NOT BE WORTH enough to retire on, but this is the time to get all your miscellaneous accounts on paper. Your goal is not just to figure out how much you have saved—so that you can project the retirement income you can generate—but also to think about the most effective way to organize your miscellaneous assets.

If you have maintained an emergency account—one to six months' worth of living expenses—leave it where it is. That is, unless it's at the local bank. Unless you're getting some other tangible benefit—like a fee waiver or reduction—you are probably giving up substantial earning power by keeping your emergency account at your bank versus in a money market mutual fund.

What about the bank's money market deposit account? It's no safer than a money market mutual fund, and chances are it offers a lower yield. Banks aren't required to pay out all their income (net of expenses) to customers, as mutual funds are.

Beyond your emergency account, if you have money in certificates of deposit or in U.S. savings bonds, tally it up. When it comes time to plan your retirement paycheck, it will be important to know how much you have in these instruments, where they are, and when they mature.

Savings bonds are in a class by themselves. Chances are you bought them in small denominations. Generally speaking, they pay a fairly competitive rate of income for the kind of investment they represent: Right now it's 4.60 percent, and there are no commissions or fees involved. Although you can cash in a savings bond anytime, you'll forfeit three months of interest if you do so within five years of purchase. The idea is to hold on to them. And if you have done just that, your bonds should earn income for up to twenty years or even longer—depending on when you first purchased them. All bonds have a final maturity date; that is an important piece of information, because bonds that have passed their final maturity date earn nothing.

If you've accumulated more than $10,000 in savings bonds, list them separately from your other cash assets (they are tax advantaged) and treasure them as an income resource. If you were lucky enough to buy savings bonds issued between 1986 and 1993, you are earning a guaranteed minimum rate of 6.0 percent for twelve years. With inflation running below 2 percent, that's an astounding risk-free return!

What's more, the interest that is posted to your bond every six months is free of state and local taxes. And you won't pay federal income tax until you cash them in. In other words, treat them like any other tax-deferred retirement savings plan: The longer you can afford not to use them, the more valuable they are. You can even exchange Series E or EE bonds that reach their final maturity for Series HH bonds and delay paying taxes on your accrued interest for another twenty years.

Just make sure you stay on top of the final maturity dates of all your bonds. Some old Series E bonds had unusual original maturity periods. If you have old bonds, you might want to check to see if they're still earning interest.

Where can you find information about your savings bonds—their current value, the interest rate at which income is currently being posted, and their final maturity dates? There are several different sources: The Bureau of the Public Debt (Savings Bond Operations Office, Parkersburg, WV 26106-1328) will send you a free copy of the so-called simplified redemption tables for $25 Series E savings bonds and savings notes and $50 Series EE savings bonds.

Simplified? It still looks like a sea of numbers to me. A better choice: Ask at your local bank. Your banker will have the same tables but can interpret for you.

If you're Internet savvy, you can download software at www.savingsbonds.gov that will calculate the value of your bonds, allow you to change redemption dates, and update your data automatically every six months. It's called Savings Bond Wizard—and it really is!

WHERE DO YOU LIVE? IT MATTERS!

RETIREMENT IS A TIME of life when many people consider a permanent change of scenery to another part of the country with better weather or lower living costs. If you're not already motivated by such personal considerations, it's unlikely that how your state treats your retirement assets will sway you. But if you want to avoid surprises come tax time or steer clear of a decision that you may live to regret, it's worth doing just a few minutes of homework to find out where your state stands on the taxation and protection of assets in your workplace and individual retirement savings plans.

Withdrawals from retirement plans are taxable as ordinary income. You'll pay federal as well as state and local income tax just as if you were collecting a paycheck. (Mercifully, these withdrawals are not subject to withholding for Social Security or unemployment compensation.) In fact, irrespective of your actual federal income tax bracket, your employer is required to withhold 20 percent of any withdrawal you make from a qualified plan and turn it over to the IRS as a deposit against the income tax you'll end up paying on the withdrawal.

Most states make withholding for state income tax elective or voluntary, but it's mandatory in some states unless you elect out of it (see the accompanying table). Lucky you if you live in a state where there is no personal income tax! Or where retirees get a tax break: New York residents can take up to $20,000 a year in retirement income from pension and other sources free of state income tax. If you are thinking of moving your permanent residence, consider the fact that you can increase the value of your retirement income by choosing a state that doesn't tack its own tax on to the federal income tax you'll pay.

Legislation passed in 1995 makes it virtually impossible for a state to tax pension distributions made to individuals who have moved out of the state in which they earned their benefits. The law is one of the most all-encompassing in terms of the type of plans it covers. Even distributions from nonqualified deferred-compensation plans (the type of plan that is often created to provide additional compensation to a firm's highly paid executives) are generally protected.

State withholding rules apply only to withdrawals from qualified plans. IRAs are exempt. However, IRAs sometimes lose out on protection against claims by creditors, which is afforded to qualified plan savings. No one can come in and lay claim to your 401(k) assets, for example— not even a court seeking redress for your creditors should you file for bankruptcy protection. However, if your assets are in an IRA—even those you've rolled over to an IRA— you may not have that protection unless your state has enacted legislation that protects IRA accounts from the claims of creditors or other litigants.

Now states must also get up to speed and add language to include Roth IRA accounts, but so far many have not. As a result, Roth IRA assets can be seized in lawsuits and in divorce and bankruptcy proceedings in 34 states, as of this writing. Edward Slott, a New York CPA and editor of a monthly IRA newsletter, suggests that doctors especially, and also members of other professions in which lawsuits are common, should put off converting ordinary IRAs into Roth IRAs until states have revised their laws to provide clear protection.

However, tax experts say it is unclear whether any state laws regarding IRAs are actually valid. At least one recent ruling by the Supreme Court suggests that all such statutes are preempted by federal law.

And here's the nastiest surprise of all. If a creditor does get at your IRA assets, the money that is paid out will be treated as a distribution to you! You'll owe income tax and a 10 percent premature withdrawal penalty if you're under age 59½. When it rains, expect a flood.

One last word on matters of state: Where you live can also figure mightily into the treatment of your retirement assets after you die. That's because state property laws

STATE WITHHOLDING ON RETIREMENT PLAN DISTRIBUTIONS

Distributions subject to income tax withholding unless you elect out:

California	Massachusetts
Delaware	Oklahoma
Georgia	Oregon
Iowa	Vermont
Kansas	Virginia
Maine	

Distributions subject to income tax but not withheld unless you elect in:

Alabama	Mississippi
Arizona	Missouri
Arkansas	Montana
Colorado	Nebraska
Connecticut	New Jersey
District of Columbia	New York
Hawaii	North Carolina
Idaho	North Dakota
Illinois	Ohio
Indiana	Pennsylvania
Kentucky	Rhode Island
Louisiana	South Carolina
Maryland	Utah
Michigan	West Virginia
Minnesota	Wisconsin

No personal state income tax:

Alaska	Tennessee
Florida	Texas
Nevada	Washington
New Hampshire	Wyoming
South Dakota	

come into play. If you die without a proper will, the laws of your state could affect the distribution of your retirement assets. (You're off the hook for IRA assets, because they pass to beneficiaries through a separate custodial agreement.)

If you have residences in more than one state in the course of a year, it's important to establish a state of domicile to avoid having to pay estate tax to more than one state. Consider choosing the state that gives you a better deal, then register to vote, get a driver's license, transfer your financial accounts—including credit cards—and arrange to have pension and Social Security checks mailed to this address. It could make a difference.

FIND OUT WHAT YOU CAN
EXPECT FROM SOCIAL SECURITY

IT'S HARD TO GENERALIZE about Social Security benefits. Some of the rules are straightforward. Yet formulas used to determine actual benefits complicate matters, and some of the variables and factors used in the formulas change from year to year.

Here are some basic facts: Most American workers will collect Social Security retirement benefits. More than 95 percent of all current jobs are covered by Social Security, and eligibility requirements are not hard to meet: Your earnings must surpass a modest threshold for forty calendar quarters: the equivalent of working at minimum wage for about ten hours a week for ten years.

When can you begin collecting Social Security? Right now, you can receive partial benefits at 62. And depend-

SOCIAL SECURITY'S "NORMAL" RETIREMENT AGE IS RISING

IF YOU WERE BORN IN . . .	YOU CAN RECEIVE FULL SOCIAL SECURITY BENEFITS WHEN YOU ARE AGE . . .
1937 or before	65
1938	65 + 2 months
1939	65 + 4 months
1940	65 +6 months
1941	65 + 8 months
1942	65 + 10 months
1943–54	66
1955	66 + 2 months
1956	66 + 4 months
1957	66 + 6 months
1958	66 + 8 months
1959	66 + 10 months
1960 and after	67

Source: Social Security Administration, 1999.

ing on when you were born, full benefits may kick in at 65, 66, or 67 (see the accompanying table). You can continue to boost your benefits by working until you're 70. Beyond 70, if you don't start collecting Social Security you're throwing away money that you won't ever recover.

How much are you entitled to receive? The formula used to determine your monthly benefit looks at your highest thirty-five years of earnings and adjusts them to account for inflation over your working years. The earnings portion of the formula figures far more heavily into the equation than the number of years you put into the system.

In general, the higher your income, the higher your monthly benefit. However, the formula is progressive, and the less you earn, the more of your earnings you can expect to replace, in percentage terms, through Social Security. For example, if your earnings have tracked the maximum Social Security wage base throughout your career—$68,400 in 1998—your benefit would replace about 24 percent of your income. For higher income earners, the replacement value is even less. On the other hand, if you retired earning $25,000 a year, you could expect Social Security to replace more than 40 percent of your earnings. In fact, today more than 60 percent of all beneficiaries 65 or older depend on Social Security for half their annual income.

Social Security benefits are adjusted each year for inflation. In 1999 the maximum monthly benefit for an individual retiring at age 65 was $1,373—or just about $16,500 a year. If both you and your spouse are eligible to receive maximum benefits based on both of your earnings records, you could collect about $33,000. Benefits for a household with a nonworking spouse are lower.

According to Bob Treanor, a benefits consultant at the headquarters of William M. Mercer, Inc., in Louisville, Kentucky, you can push your monthly benefit as high as $1,711 (or $20,532 a year) by postponing retirement until you're 70. Your spouse won't get an equivalent boost while you're living, but the higher benefit will be reflected in the payment to your surviving spouse when you pass away. However, the increase is not much of an incentive when you figure that you would have to live for another twenty years before you made up the more than $82,000 you might have collected during the five years between 65 and 70.

As you count down to retirement, you should request an estimate of your monthly Social Security benefits. Call the Social Security Administration at 800-772-1213 and follow the instructions to request form SSA-7004. Fill it out and send it back; a report of your earnings history and projected benefits at different retirement ages should arrive within a month.

When you are ready to receive benefits, you must apply for them. You can go to your local Social Security office, but it's easy enough to apply over the phone by calling the same toll-free number you used to request your benefits estimate. A word of advice: Don't expect your request to be processed overnight. Give yourself three to six months' lead time before your retirement date.

RETIREMENT

Countdown

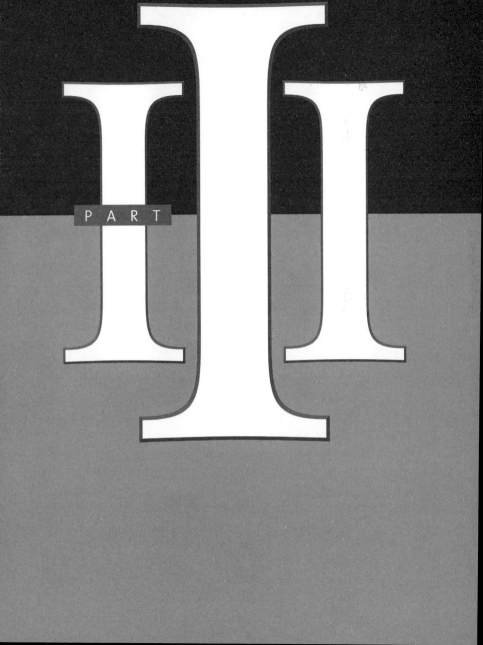

PART II

CHAPTER

4

The BIG
Picture

FTER YEARS OF putting money away for the single most important financial goal of your life, you are now faced with the single most important financial *decision* of your life: what to do with your retirement plan savings. As you count down to your last day on the job, you will be asked to make decisions about the money you—and, in many instances, your employer—have set aside over the years. As you think about your retirement income, you will also have to consider how and when to tap your individual savings and Social Security.

At work, you will be given choices and, hopefully, some resources to guide your decisions. Your employer may sponsor a seminar or workshop that focuses specifically on the topic of taking money from your retirement plans. You may receive information booklets that discuss the pros and cons of your options. Some companies even hire financial plan-

ning firms that offer face-to-face personalized investment counseling.

The problem? Getting objective advice. Chances
are the information you receive at work will come
from one or more of the financial companies that
manage your retirement funds. The information they
provide is a way to get in front of you to pitch their
products and services. That doesn't mean the information is bad. In fact, some companies do a very good
job of laying out your options. For example, Fidelity
Investments and T. Rowe Price have spent millions of
dollars on seminar programs for companies, schools,
hospitals, and other nonprofit organizations. Vanguard has published *Investing During Retirement*, a
300-page paperback book that provides a general
overview of financial issues that relate to retirement,
with companion software that lets you test various
scenarios for managing your assets after you retire.

Yet Jonathan Pond, respected personal finance author and television commentator, points to a disturbing potential conflict of interest: If the company that advises you on your choices also stands to benefit by selling you a retirement-oriented product or investment service tied to your decision, how do you evaluate the advice? "Insurance companies want to sell you an annuity; mutual fund companies want to sell you on a rollover." And financial planning companies want to sell you ongoing investment management. But annuities and rollovers are suitable for some people and not for others. And not everyone needs an investment manager. Furthermore, what's right today may not be the best choice when you're ten or twenty years into retirement, says Pond.

In the course of my work, I've observed both focus groups and seminars of people getting ready for retirement. I'm struck by how overwhelmed most people are by the sheer weight of information there is to absorb—and the gravity of their impending decisions. My sense is that they have been bombarded by information and don't know where to begin: My suggestion to you is to begin here, with this chapter and the following one.

This chapter takes up some big-picture considerations that can prepare you to make better choices no matter what kind of plan you have. It starts with an overview of the standard rules that govern qualified retirement plans. Then it provides an organized framework for thinking about your decisions and some very important guidelines. I believe it is a must-read from start to finish. Chapter 5 zeroes in on common distribution options and key considerations you should factor into your choice. You may not need to read every section of this chapter. If you have several specific questions, you may find that you can get your answers by reading two or three of the following spreads. If you master the information provided in this chapter and get the information you need from Chapter 5, I believe you will walk away equipped to make key decisions that may well shape the quality of your retirement.

UNDERSTAND THE RULES OF THE ROAD

MONEY SAVED IN tax-advantaged workplace savings plans, as well as the money due you from your employer's pension plan, is governed by a fairly standard set of withdrawal rules. Of course, there are notable exceptions. But here are the basics.

RETIREMENT AGE

GENERALLY SPEAKING, your retirement savings are available to you penalty-free once you've reached age 59½. But you won't be *required* to take anything until you're 70½. The years in between have been deemed "retirement years" by the IRS. However, you have to wonder why they chose such a narrow definition when the Americans who retire before 59½ and who are living well beyond 70½ outnumber those who fall in between.

WITHDRAWAL OPTIONS

Take it. When you retire, you can take an out-and-out withdrawal of some or all of the money in your savings plans. If it's not a full withdrawal, most companies will restrict how often you can have access to the money you leave behind. Transactions cost them money.

Leave it. You can usually leave your savings in your employer's plans until you're 65 as long as the total amounts to at least $5,000. You may be able to leave it longer by turning it into systematic withdrawals designed to meet your required minimum withdrawals (see Chapter 5).

Roll it over. You can roll your savings over from any qualified plan (as well as some nonqualified plans, such as 403(b)s) into an Individual Retirement Account (IRA) or a qualified annuity in a tax-free transfer that will shield its special tax advantages. That way you won't have to pay income tax on the money until you actually withdraw it.

TAXES

Pay in advance. If you request a withdrawal from your retirement savings made out in your name, your employer will automatically withhold 20 percent for the IRS before it cuts you a check. If you create a *systematic* withdrawal plan for yourself, or you have an investment company do it for you, you can request a waiver of the 20 percent withholding, but you'll report this income on your 1040 and pay tax on it just as if it were a paycheck.

Pay as you go. When your money leaves the shelter of a tax-deferred account, you'll owe federal income tax on it, and state and local tax if it's applicable where you live.

Pay less if you're eligible for special tax treatment. If you act before December 31, 1999, and if you take out all the money in your accounts in one tax year, you may be able to choose a special tax treatment called five-year forward income averaging. If you were 50 years old before January 1, 1986, you may have additional options, such as treating part of your withdrawals as capital gains or ten-year forward averaging, neither of which expires in 1999 (see page 109). These tax treatments apply only to qualified plans. And, you'll only get one shot at them. You can't use forward averaging more than once in your lifetime.

PENALTIES

If you withdraw money before you're 59½, you'll pay a 10 percent penalty. There may be exceptions for certain circumstances, such as disability, divorce settlement, or other hardships.

If you fail to begin required minimum withdrawals when you're required—typically the April 1 after the year in which you turn 70½—the penalties can be severe: 50 percent on the amount you should have withdrawn from your savings plan(s). In addition, you'll be required to make the withdrawal.

EARLY WITHDRAWALS

IF YOU'RE FORCED—or coaxed—into early retirement, you can get at your employer's savings plan penalty-free as early as age 55. You can get at your money even if you change employers or change careers.

If you tap your savings earlier, you can still avoid the penalty by taking it in substantially equal payments over the rest of your lifetime. In fact, there are three different ways to figure these substantially equal payments. Depending on which method you choose, you can get a lot of money out of your savings plan, or a minimum—whichever suits your needs (see page 96). You can find the tables and formulas you'll need in IRS Publication 590, or any competent financial adviser can run the numbers for you. But what a bother if you don't really need it! This is retirement money. Keep it for retirement.

REQUIRED WITHDRAWALS

BY THE TIME YOU'RE 70½, you'll be required to start taking money out of your workplace savings and pension plans if you're retired, whether you need it or not. However, if you're not retired, you can usually put this date off as long as you're not one of the company honchos—i.e., you don't own 5 percent or more of the company you work for—thanks to 1996 tax legislation that recognizes for the first time what the life-expectancy tables have been telling us for years: We're living longer. We're probably going to be working longer.

You may be able to postpone required minimum withdrawals beyond age 70½ if you were working before 1984 and took advantage of an option to choose a late retirement date under a special provision often referred to as a 242(b) election. Lou Beckerman with Northeast Planning Services, Inc., a Massachusetts benefits administration firm, says that this has always been a bit of a mystery. In order to qualify under rule 242(b), you must have signed a document that, at the time of signing, set your retirement date. In fact, the paperwork on this election has been very sketchy, and it has been possible for post–retirement age workers to cite this election and fill in the retirement date when they're good and ready.

Who's watching? It's not clear, says Beckerman. And thanks to the recent change in the law, it really doesn't matter.

If you have been part of a 403(b) plan, which operates under many of the same rules as a qualified plan, you may be able to put off withdrawals from balances you accumulated before 1986 until you are 75.

If you roll your retirement plan savings over to an IRA and then convert it to a Roth IRA, there are no required minimum withdrawals. The government's already got its

RETIRING BY THE RULES

GET PENALTY-FREE WITH-DRAWALS IF YOU ARE . . .	. . . OR IF YOU'RE SUBJECT TO ONE OF THESE EXCEPTIONS	AVOID THESE PENALTIES
Age 55+ and separated from service	Disability	10 percent on early withdrawals
At least 59½	Death	
Taking required minimum withdrawals after you're 70½	Receipt of retirement assets in divorce settlement	50 percent on late withdrawals
	Certain medical expenses	
	Taking regular, equal payments at any age	
	Rollover to another qualified plan	

tax money. You're on your own.

The accompanying table sets forth the withdrawal rules that apply to qualified retirement savings plans. The rules that apply to individual retirement plans are slightly different—and more restrictive (see Chapter 8). Keep in mind that the rules are current as of this writing. Almost every year the IRS or Congress make an adjustment here or there. As retirement savings plan balances grow, I believe we can expect even more changes down the road.

CHOOSE ONE OR A COMBINATION OF THESE WITHDRAWAL OPTIONS	YOU'LL PAY THESE TAXES ON YOUR WITHDRAWALS
Leave the money in your employer's plans until you are 65	Ordinary income tax on most withdrawals
Create a systematic withdrawal program	Five-year forward averaging on lump-sum withdrawals before January 1, 2000
Withdraw some or all of your savings	If you were 50 before January 1, 1986, you may have additional options: ten-year forward averaging and/or capital gains rate.
Roll over to an IRA or qualified annuity	

RETIREMENT WISDOM
IN FIVE EASY PIECES

ON MY DESK ARE SIX VOLUMES, each about 900 pages long, that discuss and interpret the Internal Revenue Code and other official guidelines as they apply to retirement plans. Not surprisingly, Uncle Sam has an opinion on everything. Mercifully, you don't need to know that much—although there are important exceptions and loopholes, some of which we'll get into later. Rules aside, here's some strategic help to keep in mind before you sign your first retirement document or fill out your first form. I call them retirement's Five Easy Pieces:

1 Maximize the value of your retirement savings,

2 Pay the least you can in taxes,

3 Preserve your flexibility in case you change your mind down the road . . .

4 . . . And do it all within the letter of the law so that you can . . .

5 . . . Avoid penalties or any other punitive measures that may limit your options, reduce the value of your savings, or raise your taxes.

In fact, just about every decision you make will involve one or more of these five general principles. Here they are in shorter form—mantras you should commit to memory:

◆ Get the most money.

◆ Pay the lowest taxes.

◆ Preserve flexibility.

◆ Stay within the law.

◆ Avoid penalties.

As you weigh your options, think of these as the Five Commandments of taking your retirement money. Think of them as a set of checkpoints for any decision you make. Use them to screen your choices in order to understand the consequences of your decisions.

But what do these principles mean to you? For starters, that often you will have to choose between time and money. "There's no free lunch," says Michael Chasnoff, a

Cincinnati-based fee-only financial planner. "If you want access to your money now, you'll give up certain tax advantages. And the younger you are, the more likely you are to pay a penalty for your decision." Translation: Maximize time, give up some money. On the other hand, the longer you wait to get access to your money, the greater the tax advantages, the more value you can build in your account, and the less likely you are to pay a penalty.

Some of the biggest mistakes people make, however, have to do with rules that govern the flexibility of their choices. And, for the most part, they are arbitrary. We'll talk about them one by one in Chapter 5, but here let's just establish this point: It is critical to understand the implications of any action you take with your retirement money because some decisions are final. It's an ugly concept. Some choices lead to dead ends. And some can whittle an entire lifetime of savings down to practically nothing.

Chasnoff, who works closely with retiring Procter & Gamble employees, talks about the million-dollar mistakes that regular working folks make when they don't understand the options. Chasnoff says that Procter & Gamble's retirement plan is a profit-sharing trust that invests primarily in the company's stock. The longer you work for the company—and the higher up in the organization you rise—the greater your annual profit-sharing take. However, it's not unusual for it to amount to 25 percent of the annual salary of middle management, says Chasnoff

In the past ten years, Procter & Gamble's stock has gone from just over $10 to $94 a share. As of this writing, it's in the high $80s. "I have clients who never earned more than $60,000 a year retiring with stock in their retirement plans worth $1 million plus," says Chasnoff. Depending on how individuals decide to take control of the shares, they could pay federal income tax on the cost basis—i.e., what they actually paid for them—or on the appreciated value— which could be four to eight times what they paid for them. Preserving flexibility, it turns out, can be worth a lot of money.

LEARN THE LINGO

THE WORLD OF RETIREMENT savings has its own language. At the back of this book is a glossary of terms you are likely to encounter as you sort through the decisions and issues about your retirement savings. Here are five that you should master because they apply to nearly everyone:

Qualified retirement plan. A qualified plan is subject to the rules and regulations established in Section 401 of the Internal Revenue Code. What do you care whether your retirement plan is qualified or not? Generally speaking, you can expect a little more flexibility (read: looser rules) if a plan is not qualified. However, you also want to be alert, because plans that don't have to meet the rigorous standards of Section 401 may not offer the same protections.

For example, 403(b) plans are not qualified plans, although today about half of all 403(b)s have adopted rules that are similar to those that apply to qualified plans. Some SIMPLE plans—the small-company equivalent of a 401(k)—are qualified, and some are not. Neither IRAs, nor Keoghs, nor 457 deferred-compensation plans fit the definition of a qualified plan.

Distribution. This is a general term describing the flow of money from your plan to you, the participant. The distribution can be a withdrawal: You actually take control of the money. It can be a transfer: The money goes from one plan to another. It can be a rollover: The money is transferred in a manner sanctioned by the IRS from an employer's plan to a qualified individual plan, such as an IRA or annuity. Loans, which are allowed by some plans but not others, are also considered distributions. The problem with one word having the potential to mean so many different things is that some distributions are taxable—and others are not. Some involve penalties—and others do not. If you're not sure, better check.

Lump-sum distribution. You take all your money from a qualified plan all at once—"all at once" being defined as "in a single tax year." If it's not a qualified plan, it's not a lump-sum distribution with a capital *L*.

Precise understanding of the definition of a lump-sum distribution is essential, because when the rules say you can do something or avoid something if you take a lump-sum distribution, they mean business. For example, if you retire with $500,000 in your 401(k) account, and you decide to withdraw the money to buy a franchise and start a new career, you'll owe income tax on the withdrawal. However, there's a brief window of time remaining when you might be eligible for favorable tax treatment if—and only if—you take the entire amount. Leave $10,000 in the account, and it's not a lump-sum distribution. There are no "overs" with the IRS.

Rollover. Here's another tricky term. It sounds like an edible—or a gymnastic maneuver. Just don't confuse it with a withdrawal. That's what you call it when you get the money. A rollover is the transfer of money from one tax-advantaged plan to another.

Annuity. This is one of those terms that people *think* they understand, but few ever appreciate its full range of possibilities. An annuity is an insurance contract, not an investment, although some annuities have "investment-like" features. The key is: you buy it. Some annuities are designed for putting money in, others for taking money out. Both types have tax advantages. There's the kind of annuity you buy bit by bit, as a way to put away additional tax-deferred savings once you've maxed out on the limits imposed by other plans. Then there's the kind of annuity you buy when you're ready to retire and you want to turn your savings into an income stream for some period of time: for life, for life with a guaranteed payout period in case you die in the first couple of years of collecting income, or for your life in combination with that of a beneficiary. And just as with many other financial products, there are choices you have to make no matter what kind of annuity you buy—choices that will determine your financial performance and the risk you're willing to shoulder going forward.

DON'T TAKE YOUR MONEY TOO EARLY

EARLY RETIREMENT IS such a compelling concept. You're still young enough to enjoy life but old enough to have put most of your domestic responsibilities—child-rearing costs, college, mortgage payments—behind you. You may be in your 50s—or even younger. However, if you are entitled to money from a retirement plan, your age may also be a significant factor in determining the value of the benefit you receive.

"The general rule of thumb is that you don't want to take money from your retirement plan if you are younger than 59½," says Lou Beckerman with Northeast Planning Services, Inc., a Massachusetts benefits administration firm. The reason? Generally speaking, you'll pay an early withdrawal penalty of 10 percent. The penalty applies to money you take from any qualified retirement plan as well as withdrawals from a traditional IRA, SEP IRA, or Keogh Plan.

Recent legislation also closed what appears to have been an unintentional loophole that would have let you convert retirement assets to a Roth IRA at virtually any age, pay the income tax due, then immediately withdraw the assets. Now Roth IRAs are subject to substantially the same early withdrawal penalty that applies to other plan withdrawals. (More about Roth IRAs in Chapter 5.)

That's the general rule, but of course there are exceptions for early withdrawals from your workplace retirement plans (see the accompanying box) and a different set of exceptions for your individual retirement plans—more about them later.

For example, if you die, the IRS is all heart: Your retirement plan money is available to your estate without penalty. If your spouse or your kids are the beneficiaries, they can get access to the money and pay tax on it but escape the penalty. If you're disabled or if you incur certain medical expenses, you can also take the money without penalty. And you can take the money without penalty if you're 55 and your employer let you go—even if you go to work for another employer. Also, if the courts award a payment to your spouse in a divorce case, the money that's withdrawn to meet the terms of the settlement escapes the penalty.

AVOIDING THE 10 PERCENT EARLY WITHDRAWAL PENALTY

◆ Death
◆ Disability
◆ Dismissal from your job
◆ Divorce settlement
◆ Rollover to another qualified plan
◆ Certain medical expenses
◆ Substantially equal periodic payments

There's one more way to get your money without paying a penalty. If you truly want to tap your retirement savings to provide retirement income, you can arrange to take regular payments from your plan at any age, but they have to be what the IRS calls **SUBSTANTIALLY EQUAL PERIODIC PAYMENTS.** Fancy terminology: simple concept. First, you have to pay yourself at least once a year over your expected lifetime— or your lifetime in combination with that of a beneficiary of your choosing. Second, the payments have to be approximately equal. You can't take $10,000 this year and $1,000 the next. The IRS is even good enough to offer you three different ways to compute your withdrawals. The formulas are designed to let you either get a lot of money out of your plan in a relatively (and I use that term loosely) short period of time, or to extend your withdrawal period over your entire life span with money left over for your beneficiary. And third, once you go down this path, depending on the option you choose, there may be no going back. Once you start taking payments, you can't stop and you can't change the amount you receive. You can't raise it or lower it.

DON'T TAKE YOUR MONEY TOO LATE

THINK OF THE YEARS between 59½ and 70½ as the sweet spot in your plan for taking money from your retirement accounts: Once you retire, these are years during which you can pretty much do with your money what you want. You'll pay income tax on your withdrawals, but you can take as much or as little as you want, as often or as infrequently as you want.

Most financial experts will advise you not to touch the money you've saved in tax-advantaged accounts during these years if you can get by on other resources. However, you can't keep this money sheltered from taxes forever. You can put it off by continuing to work. However, if you retire, once you reach age 70½, you must begin taking money out of your tax-advantaged retirement plans or you will be penalized. In fact, even if you're still working, you can be required to begin withdrawals at 70½ if you own 5 percent or more of your employer's business.

The IRS says you must make your first withdrawal by April 1 of the year after you turn 70½. Figuring the exact date is an exercise that requires about five minutes and a calendar that goes out a couple of years. First mark your 70th birthday. Count ahead six months. Then skip to April 1 of the next calendar year. That's the date your first required minimum withdrawal is due.

For example, if you turn 70 on June 30, 1999, you turn 70½ on December 30, 1999. That means you're required to make your first withdrawal on April 1, 2000. If, however, you turn 70 five days later, on July 4, 1999, you turn 70½ on January 4, 2000. You won't begin required minimum withdrawals until April 1, 2001. Either way, your second minimum withdrawals will be due by December 31 of the year in which you take your first withdrawal. After that, you're required to make withdrawals by December 31 of each subsequent calendar year.

The IRS takes a dim view of individuals who try to extend their tax advantages longer than allowed. The penalty is stiff, and the exceptions are few. If you fail to take a required minimum distribution, you'll owe a 50 percent excise tax on the amount you didn't take. For example, if you were supposed to withdraw $3,000 from your IRA, and you did not, you'll owe the IRS $1,500. And you'll be required to take the $3,000 withdrawal.

You could even be subject to the excise tax on a distribution that your employer failed to make to you as part of a payment from a defined benefit plan, even though the plan administrator is responsible for knowing when and how much to distribute. However, tax experts say that the IRS is likely to waive the tax if you can establish that the shortfall was due to a reasonable error and that steps have been taken to remedy the situation. The plan may not get off that easy.

It's always a good idea to comply with rules that carry such stiff penalties, and you should be wary of anyone who blatantly advises to you to break the law. However, financial experts admit that it's unlikely that the IRS will pick up on your failure to begin minimum required withdrawals unless they actually nab you for an audit. According to Lou Beckerman with Northeast Planning Associates, a Massachusetts benefits administration firm, there's virtually no mechanism for finding people who fail to begin withdrawals in a timely fashion. Beckerman says he thinks there are a lot of people who are oblivious to them. "If we discover someone who has failed to begin minimum withdrawals on schedule, we recommend they get started immediately," says Beckerman.

Minimum withdrawal requirements apply to all qualified plans and to nonqualified plans such as IRAs, Keoghs, and deferred-compensation plans. Also included on the list are 403(b)s, although many were around before the rules on minimum withdrawals were written. According to Boston attorney Tom Peller, the money that was accumulated in 403(b) plans prior to 1986 is entitled to special treatment. Peller says you can put off withdrawals from money accumulated before 1986 until you reach age 75.

DON'T TAKE TOO LITTLE

IT'S NOT HARD TO SEE the reasoning behind the required minimum withdrawal rules. Without them, individuals who could afford to live in retirement without tapping their tax-advantaged retirement savings could keep the money growing until they died—then pass it on to the next generation. So what? This example may help shed some light on the kind of excess wealth-building the IRS wanted to prevent. Consider that $10,000 invested when you are 30, compounding at 9 percent tax-deferred, would be worth $314,000 at 70½, when today's rules would require you to begin withdrawals. An attractive amount. However, left to grow another twenty years (if you lived to be 90), after which it passed into your estate, your modest investment would be worth $1.76 million. Such is the power of tax-deferred compounding.

But that's not what Congress had in mind as it built a structure of retirement plan options that would be available to virtually anyone in any line of work. The idea was to give people an incentive to save during their working years and a real sense of forfeiture for tapping the money prematurely. At 70½, the IRS says enough is enough. You're retired. We'll give you a reasonable timetable for taking your money so that you can make it last and we—the IRS—finally get the tax revenue that we've waited so patiently for all these years.

The free ride comes to an end when you're 70½. Not only does the IRS define a precise date to begin your withdrawals, there's also a formula to determine the minimum amount you'll be required to withdraw. And it's not easy. Even before you reach for the calculator, you've got to make two decisions. You first have to **DECIDE WHETHER YOU'RE GOING TO CALCULATE YOUR DISTRIBUTIONS OVER YOUR LIFE EXPECTANCY ALONE,** or whether you're going to include a spouse or some other beneficiary in the calculation. It makes a difference. If your goal is to keep your withdrawals low, you probably want to use joint life expectancies in your calculation. Ideally, you'll choose a younger beneficiary, which can help you keep your minimum withdrawals even lower.

And you have to **CHOOSE A METHOD FOR RECALCULATING YOUR LIFE EXPECTANCY** because each year you have to figure out a new minimum withdrawal. You can simply take your life expectancy from an official IRS table and use it as the divisor each year to figure out how much to take from your account. If, for example, your life expectancy is 12 years, and you have $120,000 in an IRA, you'll have to take $10,000 from your account this year. Next year, you'll divide the amount in your account by 11, and so on. That's the fastest way to get assets out of your account. Or you can recalculate your life expectancy each year, on the theory that your prospects for longevity rise for each year you put behind you. There are tables in IRS Publication 590 to help you with either calculation.

The penalties for taking too little from your retirement accounts once you're past 70½ are the same as those for failing to take them in a timely fashion: a 50 percent excise tax on the amount you should have withdrawn, and being forced to make your minimum withdrawal.

Almost all tax-advantaged accounts are subject to minimum withdrawals: 401(k)s, 403(b)s, Keoghs, 457 deferred-compensation plans, and most IRAs—traditional, SEP, and SIMPLE. But not Roth IRAs. You can aggregate your IRAs and also all your tax-sheltered annuity 403(b)s to determine your minimum withdrawals and take them from one, any, or all your accounts. The IRS doesn't care. Its focus is on the amount and the timing of your withdrawals. However, if you have more than one qualified plan—401(k)s that you've left at previous employers, for example—you must calculate and make minimum withdrawals from each one, says Tom Hohl, an attorney and vice president at Fidelity Institutional Retirement Services Company. (For more information on required minimum distributions see Chapter 10.)

DON'T TAKE TOO MUCH

THANKS TO THE 1997 tax act, you can't be penalized by the IRS for taking too much money each year from your retirement savings plans: The 15 percent excise tax once levied when individuals made big withdrawals from certain retirement accounts went out the window with a host of other retirement tax modifications.

But that's not to say that you can't take too much for your own good. In fact, finding a reasonable withdrawal strategy is one of the major challenges facing retirees who rely on their retirement savings to provide a big chunk of their regular income. Your *minimum* withdrawals are defined by the IRS, but you're left to rely on your own judgment to determine the *upper* limit.

Opinions vary among financial experts as to how to define "too much." In their book *Investing During Retirement*, the folks at Vanguard point out that you may be able to draw down as much as 8 percent of your assets if you're

HOW LONG WILL YOUR RETIREMENT ASSETS LAST?

ANNUAL WITHDRAWAL RATE	AVERAGE ANNUAL TOTAL RETURN									
	1%	2%	3%	4%	5%	6%	7%	8%	9%	10%
15%	6	7	7	7	8	8	9	9	10	11
14%	7	7	8	8	9	9	10	11	11	13
13%	8	8	8	9	9	10	11	12	13	15
12%	8	9	9	10	11	11	12	14	16	18
11%	9	10	10	11	12	13	14	16	19	25
10%	10	11	12	13	14	15	17	20	26	
9%	11	12	13	14	16	18	22	28		
8%	13	14	15	17	20	23	30			
7%	15	16	18	21	25	33				
6%	18	20	23	28	36					
5%	22	25	30	41						

YEARS YOUR ASSETS WILL LAST

averaging an 8 percent return on your investments, as you can see in the table. However, that withdrawal strategy has an important acknowledged limitation: it assumes that you'll continue to withdraw the same amount each year that you're retired.

Scott Kuldell, a quantitative analyst at Fidelity, takes a far more conservative view based on the assumption that you'll need to raise your real dollar withdrawals over time to make up for inflation. Kuldell suggests that you keep up to 70 percent of your portfolio in stocks and that you draw out no more than 4 percent of your retirement savings each year to give yourself a 100 percent probability of not outliving your retirement assets.

One of the least effective strategies is to spend what you earn on your investments. Don't assume that you're okay taking the interest paid by your bonds or bond funds and dividends paid by your stocks or stock funds, and equating that with your annual income. This strategy will leave you short of income during years when either one or the other hits a dry spell—and it may give you a false sense of prosperity during years when performance is strong. "It really is important to decouple your investment strategy and your income strategy to avoid taking too much from your retirement savings too soon," says Fidelity's Steve Mitchell, who has spent more than twenty-five years studying retirement issues.

Choosing a withdrawal strategy that avoids taking too much from your retirement savings is also a tax matter. If you need access to a significant chunk of money in any one year—for a special purchase, to help your kids buy their first home, or for an unexpected medical bill—think about taking it from your taxable savings first. Remember that every withdrawal you make from your tax-deferred savings is reportable income. When you add it to any pension income you receive, a bigger-than-usual withdrawal could push you up into a higher tax bracket. It could even lower your Social Security benefit by subjecting some of it to federal income tax.

TAP YOUR TAXABLE SAVINGS FIRST

IT SEEMS OBVIOUS: If you want to get the most out of your tax-deferred investments, you should spend down your taxable savings—in fact you should probably exhaust your taxable savings before you ever withdraw a penny from a tax-advantaged retirement account.

Consider this example: Say you have $100,000 in tax-deferred savings and $100,000 in taxable accounts. You'd like to take $10,000 from your portfolio to supplement your Social Security and pension income in the first year of retirement. But with an eye on inflation, you'd like to be able to increase your original withdrawal by 4 percent each year to preserve your purchasing power. Your investments average a 7 percent return and your combined state and federal income tax rate is 31 percent (see the accompanying table).

WIN OR LOSE? IT DEPENDS ON THE ACCOUNT YOU CHOOSE

	WITHDRAWALS	TAXES PAID OVER FIVE-YEAR PERIOD	ACCOUNT VALUE AFTER FIVE YEARS		
			TAXABLE	TAX-DEFERRED	TOTAL
Scenario One: Take annual withdrawals from taxable retirement savings	$54,163	$8,293	$65,500	$140,255	$205,755
Scenario Two: Take annual withdrawals from tax-deferred retirement savings	$78,494	$36,212	$126,675	$44,167	$170,842

Notes: Beginning account value: $100,000. Expected inflation: 4 percent. Expected investment return: 7 percent. Combined state and federal tax rate: 31 percent.

If you tap your taxable account first, you actually end up with more money after five years: The combined value of your accounts would be approximately $205,755. And that's after you've withdrawn a total of $54,163 and paid taxes of $8,293.

What if you had made your annual withdrawals from your tax-deferred accounts instead? For starters, you would have had to withdraw a larger sum each year to get the same level of income, since withdrawals from tax-deferred accounts are taxed as ordinary income. That means you would have to withdraw $14,492 in the first year in order to net out a $10,000 withdrawal. The rest goes to taxes. (You've already paid taxes on the money in your taxable accounts. You pay only current tax on your investment earnings.) Each year that figure would rise, and in the fifth year you would withdraw nearly $17,000.

The difference after five years is sobering. The value of your combined accounts would be $170,842—$34,913 or 17 percent less than if you had tapped your taxable savings first.

Of course, eventually you have to begin withdrawals from your tax-deferred accounts. But if you retire at 60 or 65 and you can afford to put them off until you are age 70½, you will have gotten the most you can get out of tax-deferred compounding.

Is there an exception to this rule? There's always at least one exception. If your taxable savings consist primarily of your employer's stock and it has risen in value five- or tenfold over the recent bull market, and if you will not need to tap it for retirement income in your lifetime, consider earmarking these assets for charity or for your heirs. Depending on the size of your estate, they could generate a federal estate tax liability, which you can avoid by giving them to charity. Give them to your heirs, and they will receive a stepped-up cost basis which can minimize the capital gains tax they will owe if they sell them down the road.

DEVELOP A GAME PLAN
WITH YOUR SPOUSE

MORE THAN HALF OF ALL Americans are married when they retire. But the cruel reality for most couples is that one spouse will live out retirement alone. That's not the only reason to launch into retirement with a joint game plan, but it's enough on its own. First, it's important to understand what you *must* do. Then, consider what you *should* do.

The pattern of legislation and tax code amendments dating back to 1974 suggests that Congress considers both partners in a marriage to have certain individual rights to their own retirement savings as well as some legitimate claim on the other's retirement benefits. Here's what that means: If you have put away your own retirement savings in a plan sponsored by your employer, or if you've saved money on your own in an IRA or Keogh Plan, legally the money belongs to you. But some or all of your savings could be—and very well may be—awarded to your spouse if you split up.

If you are covered under your employer's defined benefit plan and you are entitled to a monthly or annual pension payout, the law takes a stronger stand. You're required to take your spouse's future needs into consideration when you select a payout option. In fact, by law, you must elect to receive your benefits under a joint and survivor option, which will provide income that extends beyond your own lifetime to cover your spouse's lifetime as well.

Most employers offer a choice of joint and survivor options. You can collect a maximum benefit during your lifetime, and your spouse will continue to receive a percentage after you die—say 50 percent or 75 percent. Or you can elect to receive a level payment over both your lifetimes, understanding that it will be lower than if you had chosen to receive the maximum payout for yourself.

The federal law on this matter has more than one purpose. It's meant, of course, to prevent a faithless spouse from depriving his or her partner of a benefit that could be critical to future support. But it's also a way of making sure that both partners understand the risk of choosing a payout that covers only one spouse: Specifically, that when you die, your pension income from a defined benefit plan dies with you whether you are one year, five years, or twenty-five years into retirement.

There is an out. Your spouse must give the OK in writing in order for you to choose an alternate payout option— either a single-life annuity or a lump-sum payment, if it's available to you. Taken as a single-life annuity, your monthly benefit may be significantly higher than it would be as a joint and survivor payout. And a lump-sum payment is likely to be a significant chunk of money, which may be attractive (or at least tempting).

But your spouse's decision is also subject to reconsideration. He or she may approve an alternate option during your working years, then have a change of heart before your benefits commence.

Your spouse can also waive the right to claim part of your benefit and give the OK for you to name someone else as the beneficiary of your retirement assets—your children, for example. But there's a safeguard built into this rule, too. If you change beneficiaries, you have to secure your spouse's written approval again.

If both you and your spouse have retirement savings, it's important to coordinate decisions about your plans irrespective of the laws requiring you to do so. That means balancing your investment mix, projecting the impact of your required minimum distributions—especially if there is a significant age difference between you—and timing the flow of income from your various plans. Like chief executives of a company, you and your partner have assets, accounts, entitlements, taxes, and obligations to plan for. You may decide to share the executive powers or divide them. But you're not likely to maximize your benefits unless you take a joint approach.

WEIGH EARLY RETIREMENT
OFFERS CAREFULLY

AS I WAS GROWING UP, it was virtually unthinkable that a company like IBM or Kodak would ever let workers go. Yet today downsizing has become a way of life for corporate America. And so has the notion of early retirement.

Should you take an offer of early retirement? A lot depends on the nature of the offer and whether you see it as a bonus for leaving your employer and finding another job, or a real opportunity to retire ahead of schedule.

Your employer may make it attractive to leave your job well before you've reached normal retirement age by offering you a package that might include a cash severance payment, plus an extension of paid medical benefits and life and disability insurance. If you've met the requirements for vesting in your employer's pension or retirement savings plans, you'll also be entitled to those benefits when you reach normal retirement age. In fact, you may be able to tote your retirement savings with you in the form of a rollover IRA, a rollover to another employer's retirement plan, or a lump-sum distribution of the accrued value of your benefits to date.

This type of early retirement offer is most attractive to workers who feel confident that they can come out ahead because they expect to land another job, like my friend and tournament bridge teammate Paul Simon, who opted for early retirement from the Food and Drug Administration at age 45. He receives a monthly annuity that's 10 percent less than he would have received at age 55. However, today Paul runs a successful consultancy, continues to save on his own for his "real" retirement, and views his annuity as a nice monthly bonus.

If you have a similar situation, the biggest decisions you'll face are what to do with your retirement accounts, if you have more than one option (see Chapter 5), and how to deal with a higher tax bill if you receive severance pay. You'll have to add it to your regular income, which could easily put you into a higher federal income tax bracket in the year you receive it, thereby reducing the value of your extra pay.

However, if you are serious about a truly early retirement, it's vital to be able to project your income well into the future. There is a way to tap your retirement savings without paying a penalty if you're younger than 55—the age at which you'd ordinarily be entitled to do so if you're separated from service by your employer. But once you start, you must keep taking the money out. This is one of those irrevocable decisions that you should understand fully before you make it (see page 96).

The most challenging early retirement offer is the one that finds you just a few years away from the time you would have retired on your own—say age 55 or 60. At that age, you can begin withdrawals from any of your retirement accounts without penalty if you're severed from the company. In addition, your employer is likely to sweeten the offer of a cash-and-benefits severance package by enhancing your future monthly pension payout to make up for the years you won't be spending on the job. Or you might be offered the alternative of a lump-sum distribution.

Every year David Foster, a Cincinnati fee-only financial adviser, helps workers from the area's big manufacturing companies evaluate such offers. If it's a choice between a monthly payout or a lump-sum distribution, Foster consults the mortality tables for the client's life expectancy to help him figure out the interest rate the employer has used to arrive at the lump-sum offer. The lower the interest rate used to calculate the lump-sum offer, the higher the payout. If Foster feels his client can do better taking the lump sum and investing it in a diversified portfolio of stocks and bonds, he typically advises them to take it.

WEIGH EARLY WITHDRAWAL
OPTIONS CAREFULLY

GENERALLY SPEAKING, you must be 59½ to gain access to your retirement savings free and clear of penalty, unless you qualify under an exception (see page 76). However, the law recognizes that more and more employers are using early retirement to prune their ranks of the most highly compensated employees. In an attempt to give more workers access to their retirement savings, it allows for a special category of people: those separated from their jobs at 55 or older. It may only be a matter of four and a half years; but if you're 55, you know that it can be difficult to replace a well-paid position. And besides, you may be ready to retire.

If that's your situation, just understand that although the IRS has been generous in some ways, there are still some obstacles to getting at your money free and clear and severe penalties for not following the rules. You can collect pension income if it's owed to you—no problem. You can also take money from your 401(k), profit-sharing, or other tax-advantaged workplace retirement savings plan—but only within the rules of the plan itself. And therein lies the rub: If your employer doesn't offer you the option of systematic withdrawals from your plans, or in fact limits you to a one-time withdrawal after you've left the company, you could find it difficult to meet your income needs. Of course, you could roll your 401(k) over to an IRA, and that would give you withdrawal flexibility. But if you're not 59½, you'll be liable for a 10 percent withdrawal penalty, which seems like a very high price to pay to structure an income plan to your liking.

In fact, your best shot for avoiding the 10 percent early withdrawal penalty and getting access to your money on your terms may be to opt for what's technically referred to as **SUBSTANTIALLY EQUAL PAYMENTS,** which is an option even if you're younger than 55. If your goal is to create a stream of regular income for yourself—and to avoid paying more to the IRS than you have to—this method at least offers some flexibility with few restrictions. The rules, however, are complicated, and you'll probably need professional financial help to figure out the best way to get the income you need from your savings.

The IRS offers three different methods for calculating substantially equal payments from your retirement savings. The first approach is to look at your life expectancy, as defined by the tables in IRS Publication 590. If you want to take out as much as possible, you can spread your withdrawals over your life expectancy. If you want to take out as little as possible, you can add a beneficiary and calculate your withdrawals over both life expectancies. You're locked into these payments until you're 59½. But once you've passed 59½, you can modify your payments, up or down. You just can't *stop taking* payments. The drawback to the life expectancy method is that your payments may be smaller than you like because you still have years of life expectancy to go.

A second option for turning your savings into regular income is to purchase an **ANNUITY** from an insurance company. Although such an annuity is based on your life expectancy, the insurance company has some flexibility in interpreting its actuarial tables and will usually structure payments to look attractive in the early years—more attractive than those you could come up with using the life expectancy tables on your own. The most attractive feature of any annuity is that it offers the guarantee of income you can't outlive. The biggest drawback is that the annuity method lacks the flexibility you would have if you used the life expectancy method on your own. Once you begin payments, you can't change them—or change your mind. A fixed annuity may also be less desirable in terms of investment potential. A variable annuity would offer more potential to keep up with inflation, but there's the downside possibility that your monthly payment could drop if your investments sour.

A third option combines the flexibility of the life expectancy method with the higher payout of annuitization. It's called **AMORTIZATION,** and the easiest way to understand how it works is to compare it to your mortgage payment. When you buy a house, you know how much it costs; your bank tells you the interest rate; and you pick the term—fifteen or thirty years, for example. That allows the bank to figure out your monthly payment.

The amortization method of figuring out your monthly withdrawals works the same way: You know how much money you have in your account. The term you use is your life expectancy, just as in the first method. Now all you need is an interest rate to figure out your monthly payment to yourself. The IRS doesn't specify the rate, which makes sense because rates change from time to time. However, it does say that the rate must be reasonable. What's reasonable? In 1982, when short-term interest rates climbed over 12 percent, you might have gotten away with something in the double digits. However, most financial practitioners who are accustomed to this calculation say they are comfortable with something that approximates the interest rate on intermediate-term government securities, or around 4.5 percent in 1999.

MORE INCOME—OR LESS?

METHOD	ANNUAL PAYOUT	ADVANTAGES	DISADVANTAGES
Life Expectancy	$12,780	Flexible	Low payout
Annuitization	$29,137	Good payout, guaranteed for life	No flexibility
Amortization	$35,164	Good payout, flexible	Complicated

Source: Used with permission. *Distributons from Qualified Plans* by Thomas F. Streif and David Shapiro. © 1997 by Dearborn Financial Publishing, Inc./Chicago. All rights reserved..

Notes: Payout based on $400,000 initial balance, 8 percent amortization rate, and single-life expectancy of 31.3 years.

How do you decide which method to use? Three things matter: how much money you really want to take, how much you're depending on this money to cover your living expenses, and how much you care about flexibility going forward (see the accompanying table).

Just remember that even if you choose the life expectancy or amortization methods, which are more flexible than annuitization, you can't change your distribution schedule for five years or until you are 59½, whichever occurs later. The consequences for violating this rule are severe: You will owe a 10 percent penalty retroactive to the first withdrawal you made and you will be charged interest on the penalty. Think about that: If you began taking $3,000 a month from your 401(k) when you were 52, and at 57 you accidentally took an extra payment, you could owe up to $30,000 in penalties and interest even if the IRS catches the error the following year. The longer the error goes undetected, the higher the penalty and interest that will be due.

Cincinnati-based fee-only financial adviser David Foster advises clients to consider every other possible resource before taking early withdrawals, even though they are penalty-free if you follow the rules. "Nine times out of ten, there's a change of heart." Foster had a client who took early retirement, started withdrawing $4,000 a month from his 401(k) at age 52 and at 57 took a new job paying $70,000 a year. "Now he's got $48,000 in additional taxable income that he doesn't need."

UNDERSTANDING THE TAX STATUS
OF YOUR RETIREMENT ASSETS I:
GENERAL GUIDELINES

RETIREMENT SAVINGS ARE accorded special tax treatment. As an incentive to saving, the IRS lets you delay taxes on the money you and your employer contribute to your retirement savings—as well as on the earnings you accumulate—until you withdraw it.

Nondeductible IRAs are different. So are some employer-sponsored plans—thrift plans, for example. Your earnings grow tax-deferred, but you've already paid tax on your contributions, so only part of the money you withdraw will be taxed.

Roth IRAs are different, too. If you leave your money in for at least five years, all the money you withdraw will be tax-free. You've paid tax on your contributions, and you won't ever pay tax on your earnings (see Chapter 5).

While your retirement savings are growing, the IRS is waiting patiently on the sidelines. If your goal is to maximize the value of your retirement assets over time, it's important to understand how and when Uncle Sam is finally going to get his share—and what you can do to keep your tax bill as low as possible when it comes due.

However, as clear as the tax benefits are for money that remains in your retirement plan, once you start taking it out, the waters get murky. There are general guidelines, and some very specific exceptions. If you qualify for one of the exceptions, it could make a huge difference. I wrestled with several different ways to explain these tax issues and decided it was most useful to talk about the general rules first, then the exceptions, and finally some special situations. That's why this section on taxes is divided into three parts, beginning with general guidelines, the first of which is pretty straightforward: taxes are due in the year you withdraw money from your retirement savings accounts. And generally speaking, the full amount of any withdrawal is taxed as ordinary income unless you paid taxes on the money before you contributed it. Then only your earnings are taxed—more about that in the next section.

You'll owe federal income tax—and in some cases, you could owe state and local taxes, too. It doesn't matter whether your investments consist of stocks, bonds, or mutual funds that invest in them—your withdrawals are taxed as income. Whenever retirement money passes into your hands, taxes are withheld. Say, for example, that you request a check in your name for the value of your 401(k) account, which is worth $100,000 when you retire. Your employer is required to withhold 20 percent or $20,000 for federal taxes. If you withdraw money from your IRA, the custodian of your account—the bank or investment company that holds the money—is required to withhold 10 percent or $10,000 from a $100,000 withdrawal.

At tax time, you would have to settle your score with the IRS because neither of these withheld amounts reflects your actual tax due. It's just a way for the federal government to get its hands on some of the money it expects to collect when your annual taxes are due the following April 15.

If you have a change of heart after you've received a payment from your plan and roll the 401(k) money over into an IRA within sixty days—or return the IRA money to your IRA—you're still down by the amount that's been withheld. You have to make up the difference out of your own pocket—or you'll still owe tax on the amount that was withheld.

It surprises many people to find that a plan or account custodian will withhold an amount for taxes even if you arrange for a systematic withdrawal of your assets from your retirement accounts, or arrange for automatic withdrawal of your required minimum distributions. But with these withdrawals, you do have a choice. You can file written instructions to take out more, less, or nothing at all. It's a good idea to work with a tax adviser to determine your overall withdrawal pattern before you decide what instructions to issue regarding taxes withheld from your payments.

UNDERSTANDING THE TAX STATUS
OF YOUR RETIREMENT ASSETS II:
NONDEDUCTIBLE IRAS
AND EMPLOYER-SPONSORED
PLANS AND ANNUITIES

NOWHERE DO WITHDRAWALS from retirement savings plans
become as taxing (please excuse the pun) as when they
come from accounts that you funded with nondeductible
contributions. If you made nondeductible contributions to
a retirement savings account, such as an IRA, a thrift plan,
or an annuity, only the earnings portion of your withdrawal will be taxed. What's so bad about that? You already
paid tax on your contributions. However, if you had
known what the IRS would put you through to determine
your cost basis (i.e., the amount that is tax-free when you
withdraw it), you might have thought twice about those
nondeductible contributions.

Some accounts are more trouble-free than others. For
example, if you've used an annuity to make additional
contributions to your retirement savings outside any
employer's plan (this is different from the kind of tax-
deferred annuities that educators have in their 403(b)s or
other employees may have in their 401(k)s), there is an
IRS table that spells out how much of each withdrawal is
taxable. That's not so bad.

If you invested after-tax dollars in a company thrift or
retirement savings plan, and you want to establish a plan
for systematic withdrawal of your assets during retirement,
there's a formula for determining the tax-free amount of
each distribution. However, you may be able to ask the
plan trustee or custodian to do the calculation for you.

However, if you invested in both nondeductible and
deductible IRAs, you must aggregate the assets in all your
IRAs—that means your SEP IRAs, SIMPLE IRAs, and
rollover IRAs—in order to calculate the tax-free amount
of each distribution from your nondeductible IRAs.
What's more, you've got to do this calculation every year.
And you've got to file a special IRS tax form (IRS Form

8606) when you take these distributions. *And* there's a $50 penalty for failing to report the information. Are you ready to call an accountant?

GET YOUR CALCULATOR READY

Here's how to calculate the nontaxable portion of a withdrawal from your nondeductible IRA:

$$\frac{\text{Total nondeductible contributions}}{\text{Total of all IRA year-end balances + total distribution for current tax year}} \times \text{Your IRA distribution} = \text{Nontaxable portion of your distribution}$$

This is a nightmare calculation. My friend Fran Conti, whose rollover story was part of my inspiration to write this book, was not pleased to hear about this tax technicality. Thanks to a rollover from her previous employer's 401(k) plan, most of Fran's tax-advantaged retirement savings are now in IRAs: She has also contributed to a SEP IRA. But, wanting to put away as much as she could, she's also contributed $2,000 each year to a nondeductible IRA.

The money invested in her nondeductible IRAs is a fraction of her total retirement savings. Yet when she retires, she'll be faced with this onerous calculation and one more tax form to file every year.

In fact, Norman Posner, a partner at Samet & Company in Chestnut Hill, Massachusetts, says she will have to file IRS Form 8606 as long as she has any money in any IRA, deductible or nondeductible. Even if she taps her nondeductible IRAs to meet required minimum withdrawals for all her IRAs when she starts to make them and reduces her nondeductible IRA balance to zero, she'll have to continue to file the form as long as she has any money in any IRA. That's a lot of years—and a lot of tax filings—in the future.

UNDERSTANDING THE TAX STATUS
OF YOUR RETIREMENT ASSETS III:
SPECIAL SITUATIONS

WHEN YOU TAKE YOUR money out of your retirement savings plans, you'll owe income tax on your withdrawals. If you make modest regular withdrawals over the long term, the bite shouldn't be any more vicious than what you were used to when taxes were deducted from your paychecks. But when you want to take a large sum of money out of a qualified plan, there's an option called five-year forward averaging that may deal you a break.

With five-year forward averaging, you can compute your taxes as if you had received the payments over five years, which means you won't shoot up to the highest tax bracket just because you took a $250,000 distribution from your 401(k). You have to pay the total tax bill in the year you get your money. But the amount will be equivalent to having earned $50,000 a year for five years—a tax rate of 28 percent versus 36 percent if you didn't use the formula. Regardless of your marital status, you'll be treated as an unmarried individual if you decide to use five-year forward averaging.

In fact, you get an even better deal if you use five-year forward averaging to compute your taxes on a lump-sum distribution that's less than $70,000. This is truly one of the oddities of the tax code: the smaller the distribution, the better the break you get. If you liquidate an account worth $70,000, you pay tax on only $69,000. If you liquidate $5,000, you pay tax on only $2,500.

Now the tax on $2,500 is the same whether you took it as income in one year or over five years—15 percent. But if you have a lump-sum distribution between $25,000 and $40,000, the amount the IRS allows you to exclude from your calculation before you go to the tax tables can save you a lot of money because it is likely to put you into a lower tax bracket.

There are several things to know about five-year forward averaging. First, it's available to you only once and only if you are 59½, have been in the plan five years, and take a lump-sum distribution of all the money from your employer's qualified plans in the same tax year. All means all. You can't leave a penny in your account. Second, the window of opportunity on five-year forward averaging runs out on December 31, 1999. And that means that time is also running out on one of the options available to people who were born on before January 1, 1936. (It seems like an arbitrary date, but it means that you were about 50 when the tax laws changed big time in 1986.)

If you were lucky enough to have been grandfathered under the old tax laws,

◆ You have five different ways to calculate your taxes, including the use of a ten-year forward averaging formula.

◆ If you're taking your money from a plan you've been part of since 1974, you may be able to apply a 20 percent capital gains tax to a portion of your distribution— a huge break!

◆ You need an accountant.

Generally speaking, the size of your distribution may dictate the best way to go. The smaller the distribution, the more advantageous it is to use ten-year forward averaging. That's because you have to use 1986 tax tables, which have lower rates at the low end of the income scale and higher rates at the high end of the income scale compared with the 1998 tables. The larger your distribution, the more advantageous it can be to use the capital gains rate on part of the distribution.

According to Bob Keebler, a CPA with Schumaker Romenesko & Associates in Green Bay, Wisconsin, these favorable tax treatments are most useful for smaller balances. But with time running out on five-year forward averaging, it makes sense for workers who qualify in terms of age and pre-1974 term of service to weigh the tax implications of a lump-sum distribution in 1999.

CHOOSE A BENEFICIARY
WITHOUT DELAY

IF YOU'VE SPENT YEARS building the value of your retirement savings, it's certainly worth it to decide who will get
your assets after you're gone. When you consider the
potentially costly and disruptive consequences of making
an uninformed choice—or no choice at all—it may be easier to set aside your queasy feelings. Here's why:

◆ **DO IT NOW, OR YOUR EMPLOYER WILL DO IT FOR YOU.** Unless you
designate your beneficiaries, you will be stuck with the
plan's default option. In fact, your plan must name a beneficiary for you if you fail to act within the required time
frame: by April 1 of the year after you turn 70½ or before
you take your first required minimum distribution.

◆ **DO IT BEFORE YOU'RE 70½ OR GIVE UP YOUR FLEXIBILITY TO
CHOOSE A METHOD TO RECALCULATE YOUR REQUIRED MINIMUM DIS-
TRIBUTIONS.** If you wait until after this important deadline,
you may be stuck with both your plan's choice of a beneficiary—typically, a plan will designate your estate as the
beneficiary if none has been named—and your plan's
default method for recalculating your required minimum
distributions. So what? If you want a say in how long you
keep your assets growing tax-deferred, both your beneficiary and your recalculation method are factors (see Chapter 10).

Keep in mind that you must name beneficiaries for
every retirement account in your name: that means plans
sponsored by your employer, your IRAs (every one of
them if they are held at different financial institutions),
your 401(k)s, and the long list of other plans covered in
this book.

If there is one rule of thumb, says Gary Bowyer, a
Chicago-based fee-only financial planner who specializes
in retirement planning for business owners, it is to name
your spouse as your primary beneficiary if you want to
maintain maximum flexibility over your assets. (Bowyer's
recommendation assumes that you are happily married.)

That's because the retirement assets left to your spouse get special treatment. For starters, they aren't subject to estate tax because of what's known as the unlimited marital deduction: Any amount left to your spouse is passed on free of estate tax. Of course, your spouse will have to pay income tax as he or she takes money out of your retirement savings—just as you would have—but your spouse has several options that may affect the timing of the distribution of these inherited assets.

As a beneficiary, your spouse can begin to take regular income immediately, without incurring the 10 percent penalty that usually applies to withdrawals by someone younger than 59½. Or your spouse can roll the assets over into an IRA and claim it for his or her own, continue to add to it, and delay mandatory withdrawals until age 70½, if that's best for his or her circumstances. Finally, if your spouse chooses to leave the money in the account, he or she can delay minimum withdrawals until the end of the year in which *you* would have turned 70½—or continue to take them at least as rapidly as you were taking them, if indeed you had started taking them before your death. In order to preserve all these options, your spouse must be the sole beneficiary of your accounts.

However, if you have sufficient income resources to cover both your lifetimes, you may actually add to your spouse's future estate tax problems by naming him or her as sole beneficiary of your retirement plan assets. Here's an instance in which you should consider naming a child or grandchild as your beneficiary. Consider naming multiple beneficiaries for large accounts—and different beneficiaries for multiple accounts. It may help you stretch out the time during which your assets can grow tax-deferred while you're alive, and it may help your beneficiaries stretch out their own withdrawals after you've gone. Keep in mind that if you pass away after you begin to take required minimum distributions, your beneficiaries must continue to receive payments at least as rapidly as you were receiving them before you died.

EXAMINE ALL YOUR
BENEFICIARY OPTIONS

NO MATTER WHAT LEVEL of detail you spell out in your will for the disposition of your assets, your retirement account assets will be paid to the beneficiaries you name on each of your accounts—or to the beneficiary designated by your plan if you fail to name a beneficiary. However, beneficiary designations are not always straightforward, nor are they always accorded high priority by the financial institution in charge of the paperwork. If your wishes are complicated or your assets are substantial, it may be worth seeking professional guidance on the full range of specific options for naming your beneficiaries other than your spouse and the best way to ensure that your beneficiary designations have been properly recorded.

◆ **IF YOU WANT TO PROVIDE EQUALLY FOR YOUR CHILDREN AND THEIR FAMILIES:** You can designate your children as beneficiaries *per stirpes.* That way, if one child dies before you—or at the same time—the share that would have gone to your child will be passed down to his or her children.

◆ **IF YOU WANT TO PROVIDE EQUALLY FOR ALL YOUR DESCENDANTS:** You can designate your children and their children as beneficiaries *per capita.* If you have two children and three grandchildren, your assets will be divided equally among the five of them.

◆ **IF YOU WANT TO PROVIDE ONLY FOR YOUR CHILDREN:** You can designate that your retirement account proceeds be divided equally among *all my children.*

◆ **IF YOU HAVE A COMPLICATED FAMILY SITUATION, SUCH AS A SECOND MARRIAGE, MINOR CHILDREN, OR A POTENTIALLY IRRESPONSIBLE OR INCAPACITATED BENEFICIARY:** You can designate a trust as the beneficiary of your assets. The trust can be **REVOCABLE** or **IRREVOCABLE;** however, if it is revocable, you must be certain that the trust is valid under state law, that it will become irrevocable upon your death, and that the beneficiaries of the trust are easily identifiable from the trust instrument. If you have substantial assets at stake, be sure to consult a tax adviser in designing a trust that will meet these criteria.

There are other designations that can preserve flexibility in the face of contingencies, such as the death of both you and your spouse at the same time (or approximately the same time), and designations that take into consideration your charitable goals for estate planning purposes (see Chapter 11). With so many choices to consider, it's important to make sure that the financial institution in charge of your assets can handle your wishes. In some cases, the problem may be the paperwork itself: If the form provided by the financial institution isn't long enough to accommodate all the beneficiaries you wish to designate for an account, you may *think* you are designating beneficiaries that in fact never actually make it into the firm's computer.

Because your beneficiaries are such an important part of planning for the disposition of your retirement assets, consider taking the following steps to ensure that your wishes are observed down to the last detail:

◆ **ASK FOR A WRITTEN COPY OF YOUR DESIGNATED BENEFICIARIES** for all your retirement accounts, including your defined benefit accounts.

◆ **REVIEW YOUR BENEFICIARY STATEMENTS EVERY TIME THERE IS A CHANGE IN YOUR PERSONAL CIRCUMSTANCES**—a death, a marriage, a divorce, or a new child—and update them accordingly. Keep a written copy of your changes and requests.

◆ **ASK YOUR TAX OR FINANCIAL ADVISER IF HE OR SHE RECOMMENDS A CUSTOMIZED BENEFICIARY DESIGNATION FORM** that includes backup beneficiaries as well as instructions on how to deal with your account after you die.

Follow these simple steps and you'll have all the contingencies covered, plus a sense that the money you have worked so hard to accumulate will continue to work in ways that meet your approval long after you're gone.

MARK THESE FINANCIAL BIRTHDAYS

YOU EARNED YOUR driver's license at 16, gained the right to drink at 21, and got your first letter from the AARP the year *before* you turned 50. (Did you throw it away as I did?) But as you approach retirement, it's time to make a list of the financial birthdays that may be significant to decisions about your retirement plan money. Here are the ones that you should mark on your long-term calendar:

Age 50: Besides the AARP, Social Security may be interested in your 50th birthday. If you're disabled, you are eligible to collect Social Security retirement benefits earned by your deceased spouse.

Age 55: If you are released from your job, you are eligible for a penalty-free lump-sum distribution from your employer's qualified retirement plan.

Ages 55–59½: Although you can receive a penalty-free lump-sum distribution from a qualified retirement plan if you quit working, if you roll the money over into an IRA, you can't withdraw from it without paying a 10 percent penalty unless you can begin taking regular payments.

Age 59½: You can make penalty-free withdrawals from any retirement plan, including your IRAs.

Age 60: If you are the surviving spouse of someone who was entitled to Social Security benefits—and you have not remarried—you can begin collecting your deceased spouse's retirement benefits. You won't get 100 percent of what your spouse was entitled to.

Age 62: This is the earliest date you can begin collecting your own Social Security benefits or benefits you're due through your spouse or former spouse. If you choose to collect Social Security at 62, your monthly benefit will be reduced by up to 20 percent.

This is also the earliest age you can obtain a reverse mortgage from the Federal Home Administration. A reverse mortgage lets you turn the equity in your home into a regular stream of income.

Age 65: You're covered by Medicare.

Ages 65–67: If you turn 65 before the end of 1999, you can begin collecting full Social Security benefits. The age moves up to 67 by 2027 in two-month increments.

Ages 65–69: You'll lose $1 in Social Security benefits for every $3 earned over $13,500 a year.

Age 70: You won't forfeit any Social Security benefits for income earned after age 70.

Age 70½: The April 1 after you turn 70½ is the date you must start making required minimum withdrawals from your employer-sponsored and individual retirement plans—unless you're still working. If you own at least 5 percent of the company that employs you, you're required to begin minimum withdrawals even if you continue to work.

You must also choose a beneficiary for your retirement plans before you begin required minimum distributions. If you don't, the beneficiary default option spelled out in your plan document or custodial agreement will determine your beneficiary for you.

If you roll over retirement plan money into an IRA after age 70½, you must make your required minimum distribution before the rollover is completed.

Age 75: If you saved money in a 403(b) plan before 1986, you may be able to postpone withdrawals on some portion of your money until you are 75. Get an opinion from a tax adviser who really knows retirement issues.

Ages 85–95: Depending on the state in which you live and your annuity provider's interpretation of the Internal Revenue Code, you must begin minimum withdrawals from any annuities you own that were funded with after-tax dollars (i.e., they weren't rolled over from a qualified retirement plan). According to Andrea Bloch, a certified financial planner in Boston, this date has been a moving target. The point is, the IRS wants its tax dollars, and it won't wait forever.

After this date, at least as far as I can tell, that's the last you'll hear from Uncle Sam.

CHAPTER 5

YOUR WORKPLACE SAVINGS: Take It, Leave It, or Roll It Over?

I F YOUR HEAD IS SPINNING with terms and technicalities, you'll be pleased to know that no matter what other choices you have to make about your retirement savings, there are really only three things you can do with the savings you've accumulated at your place of work. In fact, depending on your age at retirement and what kind of plan you have, you may be limited to two choices—or even one.

Depending on the type of retirement plan you're part of, you may not have to make a choice right away. Of course, that turns out to be one of the choices. But even then it's important to understand that although there may be fewer, there are no more than three things you can do with your workplace retirement savings. Generally speaking:

◆ **YOU CAN TAKE IT,** i.e., you can withdraw it, put it in your pocket, spend it, or move it to some other account.

◆ **YOU CAN LEAVE IT** where it is. You can leave it for a short time, until you decide on one of the other options, or you can leave it until you're age 65 (longer under certain circumstances).

◆ **OR YOU CAN ROLL IT OVER** into another tax-deferred account, either an Individual Retirement Account (IRA) or an annuity. Rolling it over is retirement-speak for the process of moving your retirement money from the tax shelter of your employer's plan to the tax safety of another tax-advantaged investment account.

That's the easy part. Choosing one or a combination of options? That's not as easy. You need to understand what each choice means to you—both today and in the future. You don't want to make a choice until you understand all the implications, because you want to preserve your flexibility to make another choice down the road. And that's not possible if you're stuck with the consequences of an ill-judged decision. Helping you understand your choices so that you can make the choice that's right for you is what Chapter 5 is all about.

SHOULD YOU TAKE
THE MONEY AND RUN?

THE MONEY IN YOUR retirement savings plan is yours, and when you retire or change jobs you can take it with you. In other words, you can simply ask for a check made out to you and walk away with a sizable sum. This is always an option when the account consists of money you've contributed. And assuming that you've met any minimum requirements for years on the job, it's also an option for getting at money your employer has contributed as a match or as part of a 401(k), profit-sharing, or stock bonus plan. It may also be an option if you are covered by a defined benefit pension plan: Your employer may offer you a choice between a monthly pension payment and a sum of money that is estimated to represent the value of that future stream of retirement income payments in current dollars.

Is there any good reason to take the money? Should you ever take *all* the money, what retirement technos call a lump-sum distribution? That depends: For starters, the decision to take a lump-sum distribution from your defined benefit plan is entirely different from the decision to take money from any other account (see Chapter 6). If you have decided to opt for the lump sum instead of a monthly payout of your benefits, the next question is: What are you going to do with the money once you get your hands on it? And that's really the question you must answer if you are weighing the decision to take money from the savings that you've accumulated in your 401(k), your profit-sharing plan, or some other such plan.

The answer you'll get from most financial experts is a resounding *no:* Don't withdraw most or all of your workplace retirement savings! Don't withdraw any more than you need in any given year. You'll have to pay income tax on the money in the year you receive it (although you may be eligible for a method of favorable tax treatment called forward averaging; see page 104). In fact, the IRS requires that your employer withhold 20 percent of your account against federal income tax. A sizable withdrawal could shoot you up into a higher tax bracket. In addition, you give up forever the benefit of tax deferral.

Is there *any* good reason to withdraw most or all of your workplace savings when you retire? "Even if you want to buy a business franchise or start a new business, you should consider other financing options before you use your retirement money," says Bob Keebler, a CPA with Schumaker Romenesko & Associates in Green Bay, Wisconsin. "If you need $350,000 to invest in a fast-food franchise, borrow the money!" The interest is a business expense. However, you can't use your retirement plan assets as collateral. In many states IRA assets are protected from bankruptcy.

There is one situation in which taking a lump-sum distribution makes very good sense: If you have retirement plan savings in company stock that has appreciated significantly—in a profit-sharing plan, a stock bonus plan, or an employee stock ownership plan (ESOP)—the IRS has a wonderful deal for you. If you take a lump-sum distribution, you owe tax on only the cost basis of the stock, i.e., what you actually paid for it—not what it is worth today. It's not hard to figure the benefit: If you bought the stock at $12 and today it's selling for $90, wouldn't you rather pay income tax on $12 instead of $90? When you sell the stock, you'll owe capital gains tax on the appreciated amount, but at 20 percent most people still come out ahead.

The only way to take advantage of this opportunity is to follow the very precise rules to take a lump-sum distribution: You have to take all of it, in kind, in one tax year. "If you make the mistake of taking a small amount this year to buy a new car, intending to take the rest out next year when you retire," says David Foster, a Cincinnati-based fee-only financial adviser, "you are simply out of luck."

THREE REASONS TO LEAVE THE MONEY IN YOUR EMPLOYER'S PLAN

DEPENDING ON THE TYPE of retirement plan of which you're part, you may have the option of leaving your retirement money in your employer's plan. Defined benefit plan payouts commence when you retire, assuming you meet the plan's definition of normal retirement age—typically 65, or an earlier date if you've negotiated for early retirement. With other retirement plan savings, as long as your account is worth $5,000, you can usually leave it where it is *until* you're 65—longer if your employer offers you a systematic withdrawal option and you take it.

Why consider leaving the money with your former employer ? If you don't need to tap these savings for regular income right away, there are three good reasons to consider this option:

◆ **IT'S EASY.** If you don't need the money right away, you don't have to make any other decisions about it. Your money keeps growing tax-deferred. Dividends and capital gains get reinvested. Your employer continues to report your account value once a year (at minimum) and may let you check on fund values and account balances by telephone and move money from one fund to another. Especially if you are satisfied with the investment options your former employer offers and you don't see yourself as an active investor, it's nice to know you can do nothing until you have something better to do.

◆ **IT PRESERVES YOUR FUTURE FLEXIBILITY.** If you don't need your money immediately, or if you are stuck trying to decide among your choices, you keep all future options open by leaving your retirement savings where they are. That's a lot more important than it might seem. Prudent stewardship of your retirement assets is as much about staying flexible as it is about investment performance or tax consequences. "The last thing you want is to make a premature decision about your retirement savings and find out you can't go back and reclaim the flexibility you had at the outset," says Steve Mitchell, a retirement expert and senior vice president at Fidelity Investments.

In fact, employers may offer flexibility where you least expect it—and limit it where you most expect it. John Doyle, vice president of T. Rowe Price Retirement Plan Services, says some companies actually let you continue to borrow from your 401(k) plan after you've left the company. But if you want to withdraw the money, you're not likely to get access more than once. "Once you decide you want your money, most employers will require that you take all of it," says Doyle.

◆ **IT MAY BE THE SAFEST PLACE FOR YOUR SAVINGS.** Not safe as in protected from market forces. No one can really do that for you. However, it turns out that there's special protection afforded to retirement savings in qualified plans (remember, qualified plans have a specific definition; see page 80): Creditors or litigants can't get at them. Now that might not be reason enough to leave your money in your workplace savings plan, but in an increasingly litigious society, it's an entry in the plus column.

Although most employers will let you leave your money in their plans, there's really nothing in it for them. That's why you should think twice before you accept an offer to create a systematic withdrawal plan that would allow you to withdraw your assets little by little—which, of course, you'll be required to do after you're 70½. In fact, technically it's not your employer who will make good on this offer, but a third-party administrator or the investment manager in charge of your employer's plan.

There's nothing dubious about this option. However, once you've decided to start systematic withdrawals, it may be time to cut the ties with your former employer, roll your assets over into an IRA, and choose a financial institution based on the criterion most important to you. Because as long as your retirement income is tied up with your former employer, you've got two institutions to keep an eye on. Get your employer out of the middle and you'll cut your surveillance in half.

FOUR REASONS NOT TO LEAVE YOUR SAVINGS IN YOUR EMPLOYER'S PLAN

I'M NOT COUNTING THE *really* obvious reasons, such as you loathe your employer or you're moving about as far away as you can and still remain on this planet: Proximity of some sort makes sense. Calling a stateside 800 number from your retirement hut in Peru seems like a stretch. However, there are some other very good reasons not to leave your savings in your employer's plan, and they range from personal to practical. Consider an alternative to leaving your savings in your employer's plan if:

◆ **YOU HAVE ANY MISGIVINGS** about your employer. I don't mean the financial solvency of your employer. Defined benefit plans are actually insured. Defined contribution plans have some other safeguards—although not enough, according to Lou Beckerman, with Northeast Planning Services, Inc., a Massachusetts benefits administration firm that does a lot of work with small and medium-sized company plans. However, if you don't have easy, ongoing access to information about your savings; if you don't get quick, accurate answers to your questions; or if you feel any uncertainty at all regarding your employer's ability to make good on the services you've been promised, you should consider another option for your savings.

◆ **YOU WANT TO BE A MORE ACTIVE MANAGER OF YOUR INVESTMENTS.** Most employers will impose some restrictions. You may be limited as to the number of exchanges you can make among investment options. Your access to investment options may be limited to a smaller number of funds than those from which active employees can choose. However, if you get the feeling that the hurdles have been designed specifically to discourage you from actively managing the money in your employer's plan, it's probably time to consider another option.

Here's an example—you be the judge. Recently I decided that I needed more diversification for a 401(k) account I had left with a former employer. I spent a considerable amount of time figuring out how to take my six-figure balance from two funds to six, and I was all ready with the instructions when the benefits representative informed me that any exchange I made had to involve no less than 50 percent of my assets. And I could only make one such exchange a quarter. I'm no math wizard, but even I could figure out that it was going to take three quarters to get my account where I wanted it. The representative offered to send me forms to request a rollover to an IRA. I got the message.

◆ **THE FEES SEEM HIGH.** Tom Hohl, an attorney and vice president at Fidelity Institutional Retirement Services Company, estimates that it costs somewhere between $80 and $100 a year to maintain the account of a plan participant. Few companies charge former employees that much, but many plans pass on at least a portion of these fees to inactive employees. Generally speaking, the more costly the plan, the higher the fee you can expect to pay as an inactive employee. Smaller companies typically have the highest per-employee expense. It's especially important to ask about the fee if you work for a small company.

◆ **YOU WANT A BROADER RANGE OF INVESTMENT CHOICES.** Your employer has the right to limit your investment choices and to restrict your access to the full menu of options offered to active employees. This may be an attempt to steer you out of the plan or it may be simple economics: Your employer may incur higher fees for some investment options than others, and it only stands to reason that you're not going to get anything for nothing once you're out the door. Or you may be part of a plan that offers a limited menu of options. And if you've decided to play a more active role in managing your investment options, rolling your account over to an IRA with a financial supermarket is probably a strategy worth considering. Finally, if a significant portion of your account is in company stock and the other investment options are unattractive, you may want to consider a lump-sum distribution or a rollover to ensure sufficient diversification in your retirement years.

ABOUT IRA ROLLOVERS

MONEY OR SECURITIES that come out of your retirement plan in any form are called *distributions*. If you borrow money, it's a *loan*. If you request a check or a wire transfer of funds to your own account, it's called a *withdrawal*. So what do you call a distribution from one tax-deferred plan to another? A *rollover*. You can thank the IRS for coming up with this marvelously graphic term. And you can thank Congress for recent legislation that has made the rollover one of the easiest ways to keep your retirement money together during the years that you move from job to job, and after retirement when you're ready to manage the money on your own.

The rollover is, in fact, one of the great innovations of modern-day retirement legislation. If you're changing jobs, you can usually carry your retirement plan savings along with you via a rollover. If you take time out from the job market, you can roll over from your last employer's plan to an IRA and then to a new employer's plan, as long as you don't muddy the waters by combining your retirement plan savings with other money. When you retire, you can roll your workplace retirement plan money into an IRA. And roll it over again if, for example, you want to consolidate it with another IRA (although you'll have to wait twelve months between transactions). The common attraction? A rollover lets you maintain the tax-free umbrella over your retirement savings as they move from one plan to another.

For years, rules about rollovers were complicated by eligibility and distribution requirements. For example, it used to be that you had to take at least 50 percent of your money out of a plan in order for it to qualify as a rollover. These restrictions were dropped in the early 1990s and several other rules changed to make rollovers a more attractive option for almost any departing as well as retiring employee. Now your employer must offer you the option of rolling over your retirement savings when you leave the company. Rollovers have also been extended to all 403(b) participants.

Still, there are certain plan assets that don't qualify for a rollover. For example, if you're over 70½, you can't roll over the amount of your required minimum distribution: No big deal. You've got to take it anyway, but it can actually accelerate your first required minimum distribution if you do a rollover during the year in which you turn 70½ (see Chapter 10). And if the amount you're required to take is large enough, it could prevent you from subsequently converting your rollover to a Roth IRA (see page 134).

If your account includes individual contributions, such as after-tax money you put into a company savings plan, you can't roll that money over. Now that's something to think about, because it's unlikely that your previous employer will allow you to roll over some of your retirement plan savings—your 401(k) and profit-sharing savings, for example—but leave the after-tax savings you accumulated in the company's savings plan behind. Most employers will insist that you liquidate the entire account. That means you will have to pay taxes on the withdrawal and that's it for tax deferral. If you have more than $50,000 in savings that you can't roll over, think twice about the transaction. It may be worth it to leave all the money in your employer's plan until you're 65, when you'll be required to take it elsewhere. A financial adviser can help you compare the two options.

What do you give up when you roll over your retirement plan savings? Your right to treat any portion of your earnings as capital gains, which are taxed at 20 percent, or to use *forward averaging* to calculate taxes on a lump-sum distribution from your account (see page 104). That's a special tax formula that treats a lump-sum withdrawal from a qualified plan as if it had been taken over five or ten years (depending on when you were born). However, time is running out on five-year forward averaging. You won't be able to use it after December 31, 1999. And if your goal is to keep your savings tax-deferred until you need to use them, a rollover is almost always a better deal.

WHEN AN IRA ROLLOVER
MAKES SENSE

IF YOU WANT TO HOLD on to the tax advantages you get from your employer's retirement plan but you don't want to leave the money in your plan—for any of a host of reasons—rolling your savings over into an IRA is a pretty good choice. It's a good way to consolidate from many plans into a single investment account. A rollover preserves your flexibility: You can roll over today and keep your options open to start a systematic withdrawal plan down the road—or buy an annuity when you're older and you no longer want to be responsible for making investment decisions. In fact, most retirement experts feel it's the best choice you can make when you first retire because it preserves your tax advantages and gives you more control over your money.

Here's what you do: You pick a financial institution that offers a rollover IRA—most do, but not all; more on that later—and ask your employer to transfer the assets directly from your plan into your IRA. The process is called a rollover, and the IRA is a traditional IRA that may be referred to as a *rollover* IRA or *conduit* IRA. They're essentially the same thing. If you want to convert these assets to a Roth IRA, that requires another step—and another discussion (see page 132).

In a sense, it's that simple. Because the money moves from one tax-deferred plan to another, there's no loss of tax protection. In fact, it's really important for the transfer to come *directly* from your employer's plan and not pass into your hands first. If it does, you can still roll it over to an IRA if you act within sixty days, but you'll be starting from a disadvantaged position: Your employer will have already deducted 20 percent of your savings for taxes—because money that goes directly to you is considered a withdrawal. Now you'll have to come up with the additional 20 percent to restore your original account value before the sixty-day clock runs out. Then you can file for a refund at tax time and the IRS will return the amount it withheld.

Of course, that assumes it's no problem coming up with the money the IRS withheld: If your account was worth $100,000, you'll need to put your hands on $20,000. Even if you can't, it's still worth rolling over $80,000. You'll owe tax on the $20,000 that went to the IRS (now *that's* your withdrawal). If you're in a 28 percent tax bracket, you'll owe $5,600 in federal income tax. The IRS will refund $14,400, minus any penalty if you're under 59½. But it's too late to add that to your rollover because you've only got sixty days for the transaction from the time it reaches your hands to the time it goes into the new account.

John Doyle, vice president of T. Rowe Price Retirement Plan Services, notes that the number of people choosing IRA rollovers is rising, and he expects it to pick up significant momentum as baby boomers get closer to retirement age. One obstacle, says Doyle, may be the terminology. "People get confused because they think of an IRA as that once-a-year, $2,000, *maybe* tax-deductible contribution you can make to your own retirement savings plan." What they don't understand is that Congress has extended the IRA branding to the rollover IRA and a number of other retirement savings plans.

The common factor is that they are all *individual* accounts. And if you choose to roll your savings over from your employer's plan to an IRA, that's the key: Your employer is no longer in the picture. In every sense of the word, you're in charge. But that's good. You can be in charge and really involved—or just in charge while you turn financial decisions over to an investment professional, or seek personal service from a representative at your local bank, or tap the information resources of the folks at a financial supermarket, a no-load mutual fund company, or a discount broker. (They're not supposed to give advice, so they call it information: it comes very close to being advice if you know how to ask.) That's why it's important to choose your financial institution carefully and on the basis of what's most important to you.

WHERE YOU ROLL OVER
REALLY MATTERS

IF YOU HAVE DECIDED to roll over your retirement plan assets to an IRA, you can get off on the right foot by choosing a financial institution with rollover expertise. It's like going to the dentist. Your general practitioner may be an all-around ace. But if you need a root canal, you'll feel better in the chair of someone who does hundreds each year—not just one.

Many financial institutions offer rollover IRAs, but there's a huge gap in terms of experience. Although many companies are currently working to beef up their rollover services, as of this writing Fidelity, Merrill Lynch, T. Rowe Price, Putnam, Charles Schwab, and Vanguard are the biggest players. All have staff trained to handle the routine rollover, but when I surveyed the companies I found that Fidelity's dedicated business unit was particularly adept at handling the complex problems that can arise in the course of a rollover. It's not everything—but it's important to know that the institution you've selected can process your requests without difficulty and has a chain of command that can put you in touch with an expert if your situation is unusual.

I also found a range of services: Fidelity, T. Rowe Price, and Vanguard, for example, will offer to help you initiate the rollover process. Merrill Lynch, however, was unwilling to get involved until a prospective client had paperwork from his or her previous employer in hand.

Here are some other things to consider as you choose a financial institution to take custody of your IRA rollover: If you're queasy about managing this money on your own, look for an institution that is heavy on hand holding. That may be a full-service brokerage firm or it may be your local bank. Most banks offer fewer investment options than big financial supermarkets like Fidelity and Charles Schwab, and you may pay a little more in fees, but if you already have a strong personal relationship with your local bank, the tradeoff may be worth it.

If you're an active manager of your investments, or you would like to become more active, investment choice may be important to you. That means you want to roll over your IRA to a company that lets you invest in stocks, bonds, certificates of deposit—maybe even options—and, of course, mutual funds. The two big players—Fidelity and Charles Schwab—make IRA rollovers very attractive. You have access to virtually any investment you might want to put into your retirement account. You'll get state-of-the-art technology and service from either and access to thousands of mutual funds at a relatively low cost.

Here's one more thing to think about as you choose a custodian for your rollover IRA: What will happen to your money in the transfer process? If you are rolling over your investments to Vanguard from an employer's plan in which your savings are invested in Vanguard funds, you won't miss a beat: Your funds will transfer in kind, and any subsequent investment decisions you make will commence from the funds you have owned all along.

But what if you own a couple of Nicholas Applegate mutual funds and some company stock along with your Vanguard funds? Your stock will transfer in kind—no problem. But the Nicholas Applegate mutual funds will probably have to be sold. The proceeds will go into a money market mutual fund; then you can purchase a Vanguard fund to replace the one you sold. You probably won't lose more than a day in the transaction, but it could take longer. You should keep in mind that there *is* a transaction (it's not taxable) and that in buying and selling there can be either benefit or disadvantage in the short term—although in the long term these types of transactions tend to wash out.

One minor point to keep in mind: Once you roll your assets over into an IRA, you can't roll them over again for twelve months. So, if you're thinking about a rollover just to buy some time before making a more permanent decision about your investments, it's probably a better idea to leave the money in your employer's plan while you're deciding. Having your hands tied for twelve months seems an unnecessary burden for which to volunteer.

DON'T GET CAUGHT
IN ROLLOVER HELL

A ROLLOVER SHOULD BE a simple transaction. Once you've selected a company to receive your rollover, give them a call or make a personal appointment. You'll be asked to fill out a form, which asks for personal data, investment choices, and beneficiaries. Then you need to contact your employer to arrange for the direct transfer of your retirement plan assets. More often than not, you'll be the go-between: prodding your employer to get the money into your new account, checking with the financial company to see whether they've received the funds, and going back and forth until the transaction is completed.

That's the process, but it can be easier or harder depending on

◆ The services offered by your IRA provider.

◆ The efficiency of your former employer.

◆ Blind luck.

If you choose to work with one of the big players— Fidelity, Merrill Lynch, T. Rowe Price, Putnam, Charles Schwab, and Vanguard—chances are you'll conduct your transaction by phone. However, at this writing only Fidelity has a fully dedicated business unit staffed with trained rollover specialists who will take charge of the process after the first call so that you don't get lost in rollover hell.

That said, you can expect most companies who are going after rollover assets in a big way to go the extra mile. For example, if you call Fidelity and it turns out that your company's plan is managed by Fidelity, they may get your employer's benefits office on the phone and help you get the distribution process going right then and there. Even if your company is not a Fidelity client, says Steve Mitchell, a retirement expert and senior vice president at Fidelity Investments, the firm has been building a database on employer distribution procedures. They may be able to look up your company and tell you exactly whom to call, what forms you'll need, and—a very important piece of information—how long you can expect the process to take. If all things go smoothly, Mitchell says it should take two to four weeks if your employer values its plan daily and processes distributions by telephone. However, it can take up to six months if your employer calculates account values quarterly instead of daily—an antiquated method, but one still used by thousands of plans, especially small ones—and even longer if paperwork gets stuck somewhere along the way.

If you set up your rollover IRA at your credit union or your local bank, you may feel that you're getting more personal service because you're dealing with an individual face to face. And you shouldn't have any problem setting up the account. It's easy paperwork. However, a smaller provider is not likely to take charge of the process. You'll be responsible for contacting your employer, getting the appropriate forms, and returning them to your IRA provider. You will find yourself making follow-up phone calls and checking the accuracy of each detail. And since this is a process with Murphy's Law written all over it, it's essential that you do so. No matter how it is supposed to work, or what people tell you they will do for you, you are in charge.

The worst scenario, says Fidelity's Mitchell, is the small employer with no benefits department, who uses a third-party administrator for plan record keeping, and a client who goes to his or her local bank or credit union. "In that chain," says Mitchell, "there is no one with either the expertise or the incentive to help the customer."

WHEN YOU WORK FOR YOURSELF
OR A SMALL BUSINESS

ONE OF THE NOTABLE accomplishments of recent Con-
gresses has been legislation to make it easier for small businesses to offer retirement benefits to their employees. If
you work for a small business or small professional practice, you may have savings in a Keogh Plan, a special form
of IRA called a SEP or SARSEP, or one of the more recent
entries, a SIMPLE 401(k) or IRA. If your retirement portfolio contains savings from both small- and large-company
plans, it's important to think of them separately, because
small-company retirement plans are different. Some of the
laws governing contributions and distributions to these
plans are different (see Chapter 7). What's more, there
are some unofficial issues that may influence your decision
about what to do with your retirement savings when you
leave a small business at retirement.

For starters, it's important to realize that although there
are stringent rules that govern all retirement savings plans,
there is considerable opportunity for owners of small businesses to exercise control over the assets invested in their
employees' retirement plans. There is no evidence sug-
gesting that small companies are more likely to abuse their
oversight, but according to Lou Beckerman with Northeast
Planning Services, Inc., a benefits administration firm, the
opening is there. Why? Because the owner of a small business is likely to wear several hats that in a larger company
might be worn by others—even by other institutions. For
example, your employer might make himself or herself the
trustee of the firm's retirement plan, whereas a larger company might hire a corporate trustee.

As trustee, your employer would have access to plan
assets, Beckerman points out. One phone call to the
investment firm that manages the plan, requesting a
redemption, and sayonara employee retirement savings.
Of course, your employer would also be guilty of a felony,
but it's still unsettling to think that your retirement savings

could be that vulnerable. And because the Department of Labor does not require a regular audit of plans with one hundred or fewer participants, abuses could continue undiscovered for some time.

That's certainly a worst-of-all-worst-cases scenario. However, even if your employer is squeaky clean, it's a good idea to take your retirement plan assets with you when you leave the employment of a small business. Roll them over to an IRA to preserve tax deferral. Frankly, most employers will thank you, because it costs money to keep you on the books. And former employees are easy to lose track of.

There's another quirk that's more likely to apply to small businesses than large ones. Some may own unusual assets in their retirement plans: It's possible, for example, for a small firm to own closely held stock, a piece of real estate, a limited partnership—even artwork or wine—in the firm's retirement plan. That can make for dicey circumstances when an employee departs. Some items, of course, can't be rolled over: No IRA trustee or custodian is allowed to accept art, collectibles, alcoholic beverages, or any other such tangible property. It may be possible to find an institution that is willing to accept unusual financial assets, such as closely held stock or a limited partnership interest, but it will take some looking.

And if you have to sell your interest in an asset before you can roll it over? You'll be subject to 20 percent withholding for federal income tax on the value of the property. If you sell it for more than it was worth when you received it, you'll have to roll over the entire amount or figure out the pro rata gain and declare it as such on your tax return. Same goes if you sell the property for less than it was worth when you received it. For example, say you receive a distribution of mutual fund shares that cannot be rolled over in kind to the IRA custodian you select. It's worth $100,000 the day you receive it but $80,000 two weeks later. Now, it's really important to roll over the entire amount. Otherwise, there's income tax due on the entire $100,000.

CONSIDER A ROTH CONVERSION
FROM YOUR ROLLOVER IRA

IN 1997, CONGRESS introduced the Roth IRA, a retirement savings account with a new angle: Instead of getting your tax savings up front, in the form of a tax deduction, you get them down the road. Withdrawals are 100 percent free of federal income tax after five years as long as you're 59½. Your withdrawals may be reduced by state or local income tax. As of this writing, twelve states plus the District of Columbia tax Roth IRA distributions.

But you're ready to retire. What good does a Roth IRA do you now? If you envision a long retirement—or if you want to leave an inheritance for your children or grandchildren—and if you have the financial resources to pay your tax bill up front, you could come out ahead with a Roth IRA conversion. Here are the rules.

Going from your retirement plan savings to a Roth IRA is a two-step process. First, you have to roll over to a traditional IRA. Then you can convert some or all your assets to a Roth IRA on the condition that your income won't exceed $100,000 in the year you convert, whether you're single or married. You'll pay ordinary income tax on the amount you convert. If you're in a 28 percent tax bracket, that means you'll owe $28,000 on a $100,000 conversion.

Why is it important to be able to pay the conversion tax out of nonretirement account dollars? Because there's no financial advantage if you have to use your tax-sheltered assets to pay your tax bill and you're in the same tax bracket in retirement. In fact, if you're in a lower tax bracket after you retire, converting to a Roth IRA can be a bad idea.

Converting assets to a Roth IRA also works best for money you won't need in the first five years of retirement. In an emergency, you can tap the amount you converted with no penalty if you're 59½—you've already paid tax on it—but you'll forfeit the real benefits of a Roth IRA, which kick in when you're eligible for tax-free withdrawals of your earnings.

There's one way around that: If you open a contributory Roth IRA (assuming you meet income eligibility requirements) before you retire, the five-year clock starts ticking when you make your contribution. If you convert rollover assets to your Roth IRA three years later, your waiting period for tax-free withdrawals is two years.

Another idea: Consider a partial Roth IRA conversion. If your money is divided roughly 50-50 between stocks and bonds—by the way, not a bad asset allocation for retirement—leave the bonds in the traditional IRA and convert the equities to a Roth IRA. Why? Because, on average, equities have higher earning potential—to say nothing of what can happen if you're lucky enough to pass through years like 1995, 1996, 1997, and 1998, during which common stocks have nearly tripled in value.

Some other Roth advantages: Withdrawals don't count against your income for purposes of determining your Social Security benefits. Withdrawals from traditional IRAs do count. There are no required minimum withdrawals, so if you set your Roth IRA assets aside to use after you've exhausted your other taxable and tax-deferred assets, you give your savings even more time to grow. You can even contribute to a Roth IRA after you're 70½ if you're working part time. And if you have designs on leaving an inheritance for your grandchildren, even a modest Roth IRA can translate into a multimillion-dollar benefit, particularly if the child is very young.

A Roth Conversion IRA is not for everyone. Marcy Supovitz, vice president of retirement plans for Boston-based Pioneer Funds, says it almost always makes sense to convert assets if you don't have to tap your tax-deferred savings to pay income tax on the conversion and if you won't need the money as income for at least five years. Some advisers believe a Roth IRA is a miracle estate planning device for people with considerable assets. Yet others disagree (see Chapter 11).

CONVERT TO A ROTH IRA
SOONER, NOT LATER

IF YOU'VE DECIDED TO convert some or all your IRA assets to a Roth IRA, there's one obvious reason for acting sooner rather than later: Since you've got to wait five years to qualify for tax-free withdrawals, it's better to set the clock ticking as soon as you can. With a lot on your mind, and a lot of decisions to make, you may postpone your action. However, don't wait too long—or you may lose out on the opportunity for good. Especially if you expect to convert a sizable chunk of money, it's essential to act before you're 70½—the date that keeps cropping up in any discussion of retirement planning strategies.

Here's the issue: In order to convert assets from a traditional to a Roth IRA, your income can't exceed $100,000. The amount you're converting doesn't count toward the $100,000 limit, even though you'll pay income tax on it. However, required minimum distributions do count. And once you're past 70½, you're required to take minimum distributions from your traditional IRA. The IRS says you can't roll your required minimum distributions over—and you can't convert them to a Roth IRA. And if your required minimum distribution is large enough, that means you probably can't convert any part of your IRAs to a Roth IRA.

Edward Slott, a New York CPA and editor of a monthly IRA newsletter, offers this example: You're 75. Your annual income is $80,000. Each year you are required to take a minimum distribution of $50,000 from your $800,000 IRA. No Roth conversion for you, because if you add your income and your required minimum distribution together, you're over the $100,000 limit.

What if you turned 70½ this year? Since you won't be required to take your first minimum distribution until April 1 next year, you should be able to convert your IRA assets to a Roth IRA if you act before the end of the year. But Slott says that the IRS has taken the position that the distribution is actually *due* in the year you turn 70½, even if it isn't *payable* until the following year. If you convert your assets to a Roth IRA, there won't be any money left over for your minimum distribution. If you hold out enough to satisfy the minimum distribution and it puts you over the $100,000 mark—you can't convert a dime.

Does it make sense? No. Does the IRS always get the last word? No. A bill passed by Congress last year would end-run the IRS position by excluding required minimum distributions from the $100,000 Roth eligibility test. However, the provision does not apply until 2005. My advice? If you're thinking of converting, don't wait until you're 70. Play it safe: Convert at least one year before such questions become an issue.

There's one instance in which a hasty conversion can be potentially nasty: If you convert to a Roth IRA when the financial markets are at a peak, only to watch them take a precipitous fall, you could be paying taxes on assets that have already slipped through your fingers. There is a way out: Thanks to the same 1998 technical correction that affects minimum distribution rules in the future, you can convert back to a traditional IRA and then *re*convert to a Roth IRA at the market's lower, current value. You can do that right now—no waiting until 2005.

It makes me tired just to think of all these possibilities. But if your $1 million Roth IRA just lost $200,000 (as many did in the summer of 1998), the additional $79,200 in taxes you will pay on money you don't have might be enough motivation to get you to do the paperwork. Or pick up the phone and get your financial adviser to do it for you.

ABOUT ANNUITY ROLLOVERS

YOU DON'T HAVE TO roll your retirement plan assets over into an IRA. You can roll them over into a *qualified* retirement annuity (so called to distinguish it from the kind of annuity you use to put away after-tax dollars outside your retirement plan). The rules, requirements, and initial process are similar to those governing an IRA rollover.

◆ First: Choose an insurance company. Do your homework and check financial stability with A. M. Best's Rating Service, which you can find in any decent-sized public library or on the Web at www.ambest.com. (A top rating is A+.)

◆ Second: Contact your employer and request a direct transfer of your retirement plan assets. Because most insurance companies are still driven by high-touch sales representatives, you will probably get plenty of help.

Your employer can also make the check out to the insurance company for your benefit and send it to you. You can also withdraw money (20 percent will be withheld for federal income tax) and retain the option of rolling it over into an annuity if you act within sixty days. You'll have to either make up the amount withheld for federal income tax by dipping into other savings or purchase an annuity for the net amount of your withdrawal.

That's where the similarities end. A rollover into an IRA gives flexibility; a rollover into a qualified retirement annuity imposes rigid discipline. With an IRA rollover, you can postpone withdrawals (if you're not yet 70½) and let your money continue to accumulate tax deferred. You have a portfolio of investments that you can manage on your own; you can even move to another provider if you don't like your choices or the provider's customer service. You'll also shoulder the investment risk for all your decisions.

But that's not the retirement some people envision: If you're ready to receive income from your retirement savings now and if decisions and paperwork seem like a lot of work; if you're far more concerned about having enough money to live on than about how much money you can make from your shrewd investment decisions; or if you want the security of knowing that your retirement income—or at least some portion of it—is guaranteed, a rollover into an annuity is probably a good match for you.

Just know the differences: A qualified retirement annuity is not really an investment. It's a contract you purchase. It's designed to provide immediate income: deferred annuities don't qualify for rollovers.

In fact, buying an annuity is a little like creating your own pension plan, says Andrea Bloch, a certified financial planner in Boston. When you roll over to an income annuity, your insurance company will take into consideration your age, your gender, and the purchase amount, and then provide you with a monthly income that is guaranteed as long as you live. This is an irrevocable decision. You can't change your mind and cancel your annuity once you begin to receive income.

However, you can choose between **FIXED** and **VARIABLE** returns (see page 142). With a variable-income annuity, your money is put into a separate account and you control how your annuity is invested. You also have some protection if the insurance company falls on hard times. However, with a fixed-income annuity, the financial solvency of the annuity provider you choose really matters. In addition, with today's historically low interest rates, fixed-income annuity payouts are as low as they have been in thirty years. A single-life fixed annuity that paid a monthly benefit of $923 in 1991 would pay about $753 today. Think twice before you lock in guaranteed income at these low rates.

One more decision: If you roll over to an income annuity, you get to select the period you're going to cover: your lifetime or your lifetime plus your spouse's. You can choose a guaranteed time period, such as ten or even twenty years. A guarantee period for a lifetime annuity protects your heirs—but reduces your initial income payments.

Think about an annuity as life insurance in reverse, says Andrea Bloch. Instead of protecting you against dying young, it protects you if you outlive your life expectancy.

BONE UP ON ANNUITY CHOICES

IN A SENSE, AN ANNUITY is a cross between an investment and an insurance policy, which only partially explains why annuities are so complicated. They have grown more complex as insurance companies add more bells and whistles. It's no longer a choice between plain vanilla or chocolate, between two scoops or three: Today's income annuity purchaser can assemble an income stream to satisfy just about any appetite. That's good, because what you need in retirement may be quite different from what your neighbor needs. But every tradeoff you make has a cost—literally. And your choices are sometimes complicated by arcane terminology: *Term certain? A commutable contract? Assumed interest rate?* These phrases pepper annuity product literature, and they are enough to confuse even the most diligent reader.

The worst way to choose an annuity is to read through a list of choices. It's too long, and you'll lose interest—or clarity—somewhere along the way. Spend a few minutes with the quiz that follows. It will help you sort through the options. Before you get started with question 1, consider the statistics on life expectancy in the accompanying figure, which is based on the IRS 1983 Individual Annuitant Mortality Table and was supplied by Fidelity Life Insurance Company. The data differ from those published in U.S.

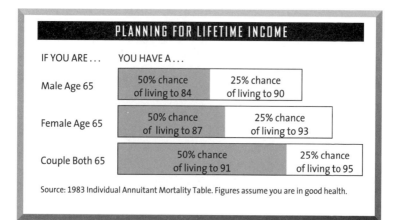

PLANNING FOR LIFETIME INCOME

IF YOU ARE...	YOU HAVE A...	
Male Age 65	50% chance of living to 84	25% chance of living to 90
Female Age 65	50% chance of living to 87	25% chance of living to 93
Couple Both 65	50% chance of living to 91	25% chance of living to 95

Source: 1983 Individual Annuitant Mortality Table. Figures assume you are in good health.

Department of Health life expectancy tables because they assume that annuity purchasers are in good health.

THINKING ABOUT AN ANNUITY? TAKE THIS QUIZ

1 Do you feel you and/or your spouse could outlive your expected life spans?

a Yes

b No

c Haven't a clue

2 Would you say that insuring income for your spouse or some other dependent is:

a Essential

b Desirable but not necessary

c Not relevant

3 As a percentage of your retirement income, do you expect your annuity income to represent:

a 25 percent or less

b About 50 percent

c More than 75 percent

4 How comfortable you are with risk?

a I get nervous about decisions that could lose me money.

b I think I can handle some risk.

c I understand the tradeoffs, and I'm pretty comfortable with risk.

5 How valuable would it be to build some income flexibility into your annuity?

a Not valuable. I have an emergency account.

b Very valuable. I like the idea I could get some or all of my money back out.

6 What's most important to you: securing retirement income or leaving something behind for your heirs?

a Retirement income

b Leaving something behind

c A little of both

There are no right or wrong answers to these questions, but they can point you in the right direction or keep you from going in the wrong direction.

WHAT YOUR ANSWERS REVEAL

About life expectancy. If you are healthy and robust and longevity runs in your family, consider a lifetime annuity. If you have serious health problems or a family history of premature death, an annuity that guarantees income for a certain length of time—say, ten or twenty years—may be a better choice.

About your dependents. If you have a spouse who will need this income to continue after you're gone—or even an aging parent who depends on you for care—consider a joint and survivor annuity. If you and your spouse both have equally good retirement income coverage, consider the single-life option, which will pay you the highest income.

About your income resources. If your annuity represents less than 50 percent of your retirement income needs, think about taking some risk to boost returns. That means choosing a variable annuity and a single-life option if you don't need to worry about protecting a spouse. In fact, it stands to reason that the less you depend on your annuity to meet your daily needs, the more risk you should take. If you expect your annuity to represent 75 percent or more of your regular retirement income, most enlightened annuity experts suggest that you think again: You may be better off combining an annuity with an IRA rollover to preserve more flexibility and keep your costs low.

About risk. This one is more complicated than it seems. On the one hand, if you're uncomfortable with risk, you should opt for a fixed-income annuity—especially if you don't feel prepared to make investment decisions, as you would with a variable-income annuity. If you're comfortable with risk, go for a variable annuity and consider an aggressive investment mix if you've got the time horizon for it. But what do you do, for example, about inflation? Some fixed-income annuities let you build in an annual inflation adjustment. Inflation is a real risk, and we know that in a period of soaring inflation there's nothing worse than having to live on a fixed income. If you had lived on the same income for the

ten years from 1973 to 1982—the worst decade for inflation since the turn of the century—your dollars would
have lost more than half their purchasing power. But
there's a price attached to inflation-adjusted annuities:
lower monthly income at the outset. This decision is anything but clear-cut, but I think that the more you depend
on your annuity for your income, the more it makes sense
to forfeit the income up front and protect yourself against
inflation down the road.

About liquidity. The feature of an income annuity that
draws the most flak is that establishing one is an irrevocable act: Once you begin receiving income, you have
locked yourself in. Now some companies are offering a
feature that would allow you to withdraw a lump sum after
you've already started to receive regular income. A good
idea? Well, that depends. The flexibility to interrupt your
monthly income stream with a larger withdrawal is an
advantage if your life situation changes. It may also be
attractive if there's a severe shift upward in interest rates:
you would have the freedom to move at least some money
into an annuity that would generate income based on new,
higher interest rates. But keep in mind that you'll pay for
such a feature by accepting lower income at the outset.
Having an emergency fund to handle such eventualities is
probably a better way to go.

About your estate. If you have substantial retirement assets,
and you want to leave something behind for your heirs, an
annuity may not be the way to go. Talk to a financial
adviser. Make sure you have an effective, up-to-date estate
plan in place, and weigh your options carefully before you
opt for an annuity. Remember, at the end of the day, an
annuity is an insurance policy. Sure, it's insurance that
pays you to live instead of paying someone else if you die.
There are other ways to achieve your income goals,
although an annuity may still make sense for some portion
of your rollover.

CHOOSING BETWEEN FIXED
AND VARIABLE ANNUITIES

MOST ANNUITY PROVIDERS offer two different kinds of income annuities. If guaranteed income is important to you, if you want to know that you're going to receive a certain amount of money each month, you should purchase a **FIXED-INCOME ANNUITY.** The insurance company will analyze factors such as your age, your gender, and your purchase amount and guarantee a specific amount of income, based on its actuarial tables, for as long as you live. Here's a typical example: You're 65, and you purchase an income annuity for $100,000. You want to guarantee income through your lifetime plus the lifetime of your spouse—a common choice. You can expect to receive about $626 in monthly income. Cover only your lifetime, and your income will be slightly higher, about $734. Add guarantees about certain time periods and the income goes down to (see the accompanying table).

However, if you're willing to accept some fluctuation in your monthly income, a **VARIABLE-INCOME ANNUITY** may put more dollars into your pocket. A variable annuity offers you the opportunity to earn income that fluctuates based on the performance of the annuity's investment portfolios,

WHEN YOU BUY A FIXED-INCOME ANNUITY

INCOME OPTION	MONTHLY INCOME PAYMENT
Single Life Only	$734
Single Life with 10-year Guarantee	$707
Single Life with 20-year Guarantee	$646
Joint and Survivor Life Only	$626
Joint and Survivor with 10-year Guarantee	$625
Joint and Survivor with 20-year Guarantee	$614

Source: Fidelity Life Insurance Company.

Assumption: $100,000 annuity purchase; age 65; as of February 1999.

which means that it could go up or down. You'll have to make investment choices—and you'll want to make sure you allocate your assets among a variety of types of investments so that you won't take on too much risk for your retirement years.

Some financial advisers think that the fluctuating nature of a variable-income annuity undermines the whole reason for owning an annuity. Jonathan Pond, the author of dozens of books on personal finance and a national television commentator, says that if you're looking for guaranteed income, go for it—and buy a fixed-income annuity. If you're willing to shoulder the investment risk of a variable annuity, Pond says you might as well opt for an IRA rollover into mutual funds, where fees are lower and you preserve the flexibility to change your mind.

Annuity professionals disagree. Says Andrea Bloch, a certified financial planner in Boston, a variable-income annuity offers a number of benefits. First, it provides a hedge against inflation. Even a low rate of inflation will reduce the buying power of income from a fixed annuity. There's also an element of convenience: Income annuities are designed to meet IRS required minimum withdrawals, leaving one less headache for you to deal with.

But most important, you can't outlive your income with a variable annuity even if you live through a period of bad markets. Not necessarily true, says Bloch, if you are taking systematic withdrawals from a mutual fund portfolio. "Outlive your life expectancy," warns Bloch, "and you could run out of money."

Understanding how the income on your variable annuity is calculated is something of a challenge. However, the methodology is not entirely inscrutable, and I'll give it a try: In addition to the purchase payment, your age, and the payout option you choose, the amount of income you receive from a variable annuity depends on a formula. And you have a say in how it is figured by choosing what is called the **BENCHMARK RATE OF RETURN** or **ASSUMED INTEREST RATE.** This parameter does two things: It helps establish the amount of your first payment, and it establishes a standard or hurdle rate for future payments. After you receive your first check, your income will increase, decrease, or stay the same depending on whether your portfolio's investment return "beat" the benchmark. Different companies offer different rates, but most companies offer two rates: typically a lower rate of 2.5 to 3.5 percent and a higher rate of 5 to 6 percent. In some states high benchmarks are not permitted.

Pick the lower rate, and the initial amount of income you receive may be slightly lower at the outset, but both the potential gains and the rate at which your income can rise are greater. At the higher rate, your initial income amount is larger, but you can expect increases to be smaller and more gradual.

Any change, up or down, in the performance of the investment portfolios you select will change the income you receive by the same percentage, minus the benchmark rate and annuity expenses. However, the actual dollars are spread out over the life of the contract to help provide some downside protection. Some annuities adjust the amount annually, some monthly.

Instead of purchasing mutual fund shares, as you might have if you had rolled your money over into an IRA, your annuity purchase buys you *annuity units*, which will remain constant over the period of time you collect income. The value of these units changes, based on the performance of the investment portfolios you choose. To determine your income payment each month, you simply multiply the annuity value for each investment portfolio by the number of annuity units you own.

Variable annuities have been around for more than fifty years, but they've gained in popularity during the bull market that has taken the stock market up more than sevenfold since the early 1980s. Some annuity owners who have been along for the ride are earning five times the income today that they started with twenty years ago. That's pretty impressive when you think that if your variable income annuity had been paying you $500 a month twenty years ago, you could be receiving more than $3,000 a month today.

And so far there have been few big breaks downward. In 1987, when the stock market fell precipitously over a two-month period, some annuity checks came down 30 percent but then recovered over the next two years. A hypothetical example offered by Fidelity Life Insurance Company shows that the income from a $100,000 annuity that lost about 2 percent a year for ten years would fall from $725 to $200. Ouch! The good news is that there's never been a decade in recent memory during which stocks have performed that poorly—not even during the Depression. On the other hand, inflation—however low it has fallen recently—remains a real threat to retirement income and one of the strongest arguments in favor of a variable-income annuity.

DON'T BITE ON THE
PENSION MAX PITCH

FEW OPTIONS THAT YOU will consider regarding your retirement income are clear-cut. This one is. It's a strategy called **PENSION MAXIMIZATION,** and it is fraught with so many negative possibilities that it deserves to be called a bad idea. The concept is often presented by a life insurance agent to a married individual who is in line to receive an annuity as a form of pension payout from an employer's defined benefit plan. Here's the pitch: With an annuity, you've got a choice between a payout that lasts through your lifetime—a single-life annuity—or a joint and survivor annuity that extends benefits to your spouse in the event that you die first. In fact, you may be required to choose the joint and survivor option unless your spouse waives his or her benefits in writing.

But the tradeoff for this form of security is lower monthly income. So the insurance industry offers this deal: You opt for a single-life annuity with its higher monthly income—sometimes considerably higher—and with the money you would have "lost" in the form of a reduced monthly benefit by choosing a joint and survivor annuity, you purchase an insurance policy on your life, naming your spouse as the beneficiary. Here's an example: Say your employer offers you a choice between monthly income of $2,000 for your lifetime or $1,500 to extend to your spouse's lifetime if you die first. The idea is that you would take the $500 monthly differential, or $6,000 per year, and purchase an insurance policy—typically, a whole-life policy that would build up some cash value—that, if you were to die, would replace the $1,500 in survivor benefits your spouse would be entitled to had you opted for the joint and survivor annuity. The idea is that you should be no worse off than if you had opted for the lower-paying annuity, and you should be better off over time.

But here's where things get dicey. Most financial planners say that the policy you purchase should be at least ten times the annual income figure you're shooting for: in this case, $18,000. Gary Uhl, an independent Massachusetts insurance executive, says that a whole-life policy for $180,000 would probably run around $5,800 a year for ten years if you and your spouse are in your mid-50s when you purchase it. The older you are, the higher the premiums.

If all goes according to plan, after ten years you would be ahead each year by $6,000. But talk about a proposition in which the planets and stars have to line up in your favor! What happens if your spouse dies? You're out the insurance money. What happens if you get divorced? Now your spouse is out of luck. Sure, he or she can insist that you continue to make the insurance payments, but who's going to pay the legal fees for that fight? And what if the insurer goes belly up? It's not likely, but at least a portion of the pension payments you would have collected from your employer are insured by a government agency called the Pension Benefit Guaranty Corporation, whereas your insurance company offers its good name and its track record, but no such guarantee.

Think about it this way: If pension maximization is good for the insurance company that sells it to you—and it's good for you, too—exactly how does it work? It works because the actuarial tables treat you as a statistic. But you're not. And it's scary to think that you have to outlive the statistics by a significant margin to collect your reward. "It's a crap shoot," says Uhl, who doesn't write such policies himself. "You're banking on assumptions about life expectancy and investment performance that could determine whether the insurance costs can actually be justified." Do yourself a favor: Pass on pension max.

NOW, THEN, AND LATER

ROLLOVER IRA? ANNUITY? Leave your money in your employer's plan? Or take the money and run? These choices may seem overwhelming when you are on the verge of making so many other decisions about retirement. However, because retirement could represent as much as 25 percent of your life span, it's unlikely that one strategy is going to carry you through so many years. That's why flexibility is probably the most important factor to weigh into the decisions you make about your retirement savings at the outset. If you're busy, healthy, and active when you retire at 60, chances are you may work part time for several years. If you can afford not to touch your tax-deferred savings during these years, living on your part-time income and any taxable savings you have put away, you can give your long-term retirement savings an incredible boost. If you retired at 60 with $200,000 in your 401(k), and you earned an average of 8 percent on your investments, in ten years you would have $431,785—and you wouldn't have added a penny.

After you're 70½, you'll be forced to begin required minimum distributions from most of your tax-advantaged plans. If you roll your assets over into an IRA at this point, you can maintain tax deferral, create a regular withdrawal program (either on your own or with the help of your investment company or an investment professional), and still have the flexibility to take out a chunk of money for an emergency or a special expenditure, if you want it.

At some point, the paperwork and attention to detail that are required for managing your assets may seem more than you want to do on your own. That's when you may want to turn the job over to a professional investment manager or purchase an annuity to create a regular stream of income you can count on for the rest of your life. The very reasons that some advisers give for passing on an annuity early in retirement now weigh in your favor. When you're older, it's nice to know that you have secured an amount of income that you can't outlive. Just make sure that you've preserved the flexibility to make the choice when you're ready: the method you choose to recalculate your life expectancy in order to arrive at the amount of your required minimum withdrawals after you're 70½ can make a difference. Choose the **RECALCULATION METHOD** and you keep your options open. Choose the **DECLINING BALANCE** or **FIXED-TERM METHOD** and you'll lose the flexibility to roll your qualified retirement assets into an annuity (see Chapter 10). Them's the breaks, says the IRS.

Be mindful that you may need to adjust your investment strategy several times in retirement. Having a cushion of stocks for growth potential certainly makes sense in your 60s. When you reach your 80s, it makes no sense if you need all your resources to generate income on which to live. On the other hand, if you are building wealth to pass on to the next generation, or for charitable causes, you should keep a sizable percentage of your investments in stock throughout your lifetime.

One way to shed some of the burden of active investment management in your middle to late retirement years is to consider an asset allocation fund. Generally speaking, these funds do not match the performance you might hope to achieve if you selected funds on your own. It's a little like buying stereo equipment. The manufacturer's "rack" set of speakers, CD player, and receiver may be good, but great is a stretch. However, good is probably good enough if you value the convenience a conservative asset allocation fund can offer to you. Pick one that's no-load. You can elect systematic withdrawals for monthly income and to meet required minimum withdrawals. And you'll still retain the flexibility to opt for an annuity at some later date.

HOW TO GET THE
Most from Your

Retirement
SAVINGS

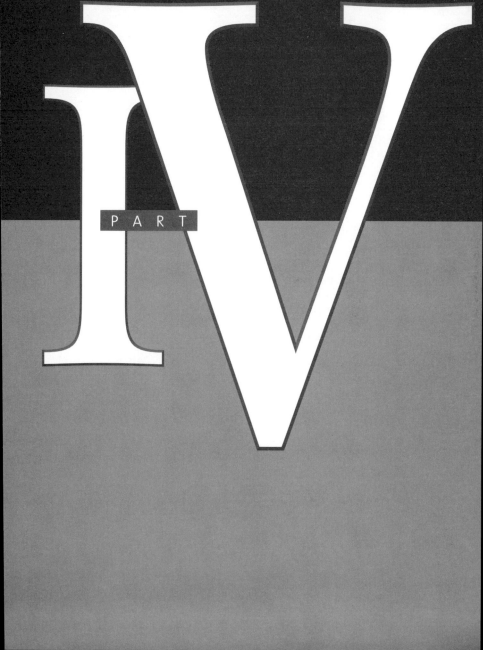

PART IV

'VE HEARD MY PARENTS compare the value of their retirement benefits to those that their friends have collected. I know that they think the railroads have taken good care of their employees and that the meat packer's union has been pretty chintzy. As a former schoolteacher, my father spent hours weighing the tradeoffs between a lower monthly benefit and early retirement and a higher benefit and delayed retirement. (Early won out; the hassle factor of dealing with unruly teenagers wasn't part of the formula.) My mother, a retired librarian, has learned how to read annuity contract jargon and figure out how much part-time income she could earn without losing Social Security benefits. By contrast, my brother-in-law Sam, a generation younger and an executive with a California-based electronics firm, has become an expert on the ins and outs of employee stock ownership plans and executive deferred-compensation plans.

Whether you are entitled to receive income from your employer or you have been the sole architect of your retirement savings program, the range of possible benefits is astounding. Yet, if I had to guess how many people actually consider retirement benefits as a factor in making a job decision, it would be a pretty small number. As you approach retirement, it's too late to fuss over what might have been. My former colleague Peter Lynch is fond of advising investors to "know what you own, and why you own it." If you're getting ready to retire, I say: know what you're owed—and make sure you get it!

CHAPTER

THE PROMISE
of Lifetime Income
from Your Employer's
Pension Plan

ESPITE THE GAINS
that other kinds of retirement savings plans have
made in the American workplace—and contrary to
what you are likely to read in the press—the traditional pension plan that promises to pay you lifetime
income in exchange for years of loyal service remains
the most common retirement benefit plan nation-
wide. Recent government surveys show that 56 percent of private-sector employees in medium-size and
large companies and more than 90 percent of state
and local government employees participate in traditional defined benefit plans.

A defined benefit plan is designed to pay you a
retirement benefit on a specified future date, either
when you retire or when you leave the company having negotiated a date to commence benefits earlier
than your employer's definition of normal retirement age.

Employee Benefit Research Institute statistics show that most people take their pension in the form of monthly income. Big companies tend to pay this directly from their own trust funds, built up over the years. Smaller companies may go out and purchase an annuity for you. However, an increasing number of plans offer departing employees another option: a one-time payment called a lump-sum distribution.

That's the big picture. Not all defined benefit plans are the same. It makes a difference, for example, whether you work for a company in the private sector, or for a state or federal government or agency in the public sector, or for a very small professional practice—a medical or legal practice, for example.

PRIVATE-SECTOR VERSUS
PUBLIC-SECTOR PLANS

PRIVATE- AND PUBLIC-SECTOR defined benefit plans are different in several key ways. For example, if you work in the private sector, chances are you have not contributed to your pension plan. When you took your job, a human resources representative or the company's financial officer probably sat down and showed you what you could receive if you stayed with the firm for twenty or thirty years. And it probably looked pretty good—especially if it wasn't going to cost you a dime along the way.

However, public workers covered by defined benefit plans are typically required to make contributions: In fact, they may be the sole source of contributions to their plans. The plans are in place to enforce the discipline of saving for retirement and to fund either the purchase of an annuity or a lump-sum distribution at retirement. And they work pretty well. Schoolteachers, police and fire workers, city and state employees, and workers at public hospitals are almost all covered by—and perhaps required to participate in—state public employee retirement plans and often by other optional savings plans as well. Federal workers, who are covered by either Civil Service or Federal Employee Retirement Services, are required to contribute a set percentage of their wages to their plans. However, like Social Security, in most cases the amount they contribute actually has no bearing on the income they end up receiving.

Another difference, which may be more significant in some areas of the country than others, is that public-sector defined benefit plans are not subject to national retirement laws that apply to private-sector plans. What does that mean to you? Rules that govern private-sector benefits plan are strict. They're designed to offer maximum protection and to exact an employer's compliance with the letter of the law.

But public-sector employees may not be so lucky. It's one thing if you're on the payroll of the state of California, which maintains one of the largest public retirement systems in the country, with billions of dollars at stake and sophisticated investment management to stay on top of it. However, you don't have to live in some backwater state to be exposed to questionable practices. In the not-so-recent past, the state of Massachusetts was reported to have plunked its state employees' retirement funds into bank savings accounts earning the going bank interest rate. Investment returns? What do you think? This practice has since been abandoned, and the politician who engineered it to stay cozy with local banking interests is long gone. But it doesn't take a genius to figure out that taxpayers had to kick in millions of dollars more to fund retirement for public employees, who in turn must have lost out on millions in potential benefits. But who was going to question the procedures? Who thinks to ask about the fiduciary responsibility of your employer when your employer is the state you live in? I guess the bottom line is that you should, and you must, ask questions about the money that is expected to finance your retirement and be skeptical about the answers you receive.

One good thing most public-sector employees can look forward to that private-sector employees cannot is cost-of-living adjustments during their retirement years. Typically the adjustment is capped at a maximum of 3 percent. And in recent years these increases have not amounted to much. But even a 1 percent increase can add up over time.

One of the big drawbacks of traditional defined benefit plans is that if you leave your employer, your benefits— even if you are vested to receive them—may be frozen in time. If you're owed more than $5,000 you may not be able to take them with you. You can't add to them. They won't grow, compound, or derive any benefit at all from tax deferral. However, for Americans who remain on the job with the same employer for twenty or more years, defined benefit plans offer income that can extend paydays right through retirement.

In recent years, some companies have taken bold steps to preserve the best features of their traditional pension plans and eliminate these negative features. A number of so-called hybrid plans have emerged that target a future retirement benefit—either a monthly income stream or a lump-sum distribution (typically a choice between the two)—yet create a current value that can be determined at any point along an employee's career path and translated into an immediate, portable benefit.

Cash balance plans actually create individual accounts that are credited with a dollar amount each year (or quarter), based on the employee's current pay and years of service, as well as an interest rate that is typically tied to the thirty-year U.S. Treasury rate or some other fairly conservative fixed-income index. Your account is actually merely a bookkeeping device, and its value is nothing more than an actuarial projection of what an account would have to be worth at a certain point in time to generate a future benefit, assuming that you kept working and your income rose, or at least remained level.

Pension equity plans are similar. However, instead of individual accounts and interest, employees get credit for a percentage for each year worked. That percentage is applied to a worker's final average earnings to determine the value of the benefit.

Floor plans are another variation on traditional plans, designed to address the concerns of some employers—and some employees—that a lack of personal discipline and investment skill may impoverish their employees' retirement years. By creating a plan that defines a minimum retirement benefit but also has a contributory component, which is often a profit-sharing plan, employers can establish a "floor" for future benefits—hence the name. At retirement or termination, the employee gets the benefit of whichever account has done better.

The neat thing about these plans is that you can take your vested retirement benefits with you if you change jobs, and they can continue to grow. In theory, that's possible with any defined benefit plan. But there's not the same sense of personal ownership created over the years: Having a separate account that has a value you can point to or seeing your percentage rise for every year you're employed has a positive psychological impact. Besides, unless your pension account is worth less than $5,000 most employers won't give you a lump-sum distribution from a traditional plan—a blind spot, according to Tom Hohl, an attorney and vice president at Fidelity Institutional Retirement Services Company. "Employers have to pay insurance on each former employee they keep listed on the books. They have to pay it every year." According to Hohl, it should be cheaper to negotiate distributions to departing employees no matter how much they're owed. Of course, the value of your benefit is frozen when you leave. And I suppose there's always the chance that the company will lose track of you—or that you'll die before collecting some or all of your benefit.

Older employees may be less enthusiastic about cash balance and pension equity plans. They feel that the formula used to calculate future benefits discriminates against them. And recently employees at several firms have taken their employers to court over the matter. Recognizing that the plans do indeed have the potential to shortchange older employees with years of service, some companies that have substituted cash balance plans for traditional defined benefit plans—Polaroid, for example—have ushered them in over a transition period during which they figure benefits using both formulas and offer retiring employees over a certain age the higher amount.

TAKE THE MYSTERY OUT OF
YOUR PENSION PLAN

YOU MAY THINK YOUR pension benefit is both mysterious and nonnegotiable, and that there's not much you can do and therefore not much you need to know about it. That's simply not true. Yes, the size of the pension benefit you will collect from your employer's plan is determined by a formula, usually tied to your earnings, your length of service to your employer, or both. But if you're going to ensure that your payment is accurate and equitable, you should know:

◆ **THE UNDERLYING COMPONENTS OF THE FORMULA** your employer uses to determine pension benefits, whether it is a monthly income payment or a lump-sum distribution. Your employer should be able to explain it in plain English. Insist on it. If you're not satisfied with the explanation—or it confuses you—take it to a tax or financial adviser and ask for an explanation that you *can* understand.

◆ **YOUR PLAN'S DEFINITION OF NORMAL RETIREMENT AGE.** Typically it's 65 (or five years after you start working, whichever comes later), but find out. That's the most common official definition—but it could be earlier, and it's spelled out in your employer's plan document. In fact, there may be different benefit levels available at different combinations of age and years of service. For example, you may be eligible for full retirement at 55 with thirty years of service or at 65 with twenty years of service. Especially if you have worked in the public sector, you should ask about and understand all your age- and service-related options. Much has changed over the years.

◆ **WHAT CHOICES ARE AVAILABLE TO YOU,** and what they are worth. For example:
  What is the difference between your employer's offer of a single-life and a joint and survivor annuity? Find out the difference in percentage and dollar terms. Some corpo-

rate plans subsidize this offering and may provide your surviving spouse 75 percent or more of your monthly benefit; some more Spartan plans offer your spouse 50 percent of your benefit, the minimum required by law, which could easily translate into less than 20 percent of your full-employment income. That means if you were earning $40,000 when you retired, and your annual retirement benefit was $16,000, your spouse would be entitled to a meager $8,000 annually if you passed away. Add that to a modest Social Security benefit, and you've gone from a relatively middle-class income to near poverty-level existence.

Can you take your benefits as a lump-sum distribution? A lump-sum distribution is one way to get around the risk that you may not live long enough to collect what you think you're entitled to. If your account value is $5,000 or less, you must be given this option. But today many plans also offer this option to workers retiring from long-term employment. The amount, which represents the present value of the future stream of income payments that you would be entitled to receive, could easily be six figures. Before you accept such an offer, you'll want to know how the distribution was calculated. Recent legislation requires plans to begin using a standard 1983 mortality table and an interest rate based on the current thirty-year Treasury bond. However, some plans may be entitled to use a different figure through 1999. And given today's low interest rates—recently the thirty-year Treasury bond hit a thirty-year low when it dropped below 5 percent—plans that can buy a little more time to use a higher rate can minimize the payout of lump-sum distributions. (The lower the interest rate they have to plug into their formula, the higher the dollar amount it will compute.)

Even plans that use the thirty-year Treasury bond rate can pick from a number of time frames, which could make a significant difference to you. Does your plan use the rate as of the end of the year? The end of the month? The average over a several-month period? This is not an easy offer to analyze.

Do yourself a favor and schedule a session with a reputable financial planner to help you decide whether a lump sum is a better deal for you. You'll increase your chance of getting a fair evaluation if you choose someone who is independent from an insurance or investment company. In fact, look out if you get an offer to do this exercise for free. Sounds like someone sees a potential sale with a fat commission coming.

A competent professional will weigh a number of factors before recommending a decision: Your tax situation, for example, may be important. Depending on your age, and how many years of service you have, you may be eligible for one of the special tax treatments such as five- or ten-year forward averaging. Or some portion of your distribution may be eligible for taxation at the capital gains rate of 20 percent. Conceivably, an adviser may suggest that you look at the interest rate picture. If you have some flexibility as to your retirement date, the rate your employer uses to compute your lump-sum distribution could make a huge difference. The ideal situation would be to grab your distribution while rates are low—and have it in hand to make investment decisions of your own when rates are higher.

Interestingly, your gender is also a consideration. Steve Mitchell, a retirement expert and senior vice president at Fidelity Investments, says that because companies must use a gender-blind table to calculate the value of both lump-sum distributions and monthly benefits, men can often do better taking the lump sum and buying their own annuity from an insurance company, which will use a gender-specific actuarial table to calculate the monthly annuity payout. All things being equal, that should be higher than you could get from your employer.

But guess what? If you are one of your firm's highly paid employees, you may be surprised to learn that you can't collect a lump-sum distribution because your employer's plan may not be in good enough financial shape to come up with the money. If you're one of those who is actually eligible to collect the maximum $130,000 annual income allowed under the rules that govern defined benefit plans, the lump-sum amount that would produce that income stream could be a million dollars. Joan Gucciardi, president of a Wisconsin benefits consulting and actuarial firm, says this situation is more likely in a small firm than in a large one, but it often comes as a big surprise to long-term employees who have watched others leave their firms with lump sums and assumed that they would be entitled to the same.

◆ **ANY QUIRKS OR WRINKLES THAT COULD AFFECT YOUR TOTAL BENEFITS PICTURE.** For example, Janet Briaud, a Texas-based financial planner, says that employees of the Texas education system can actually lose their health benefits if they choose to roll over a lump-sum distribution of their retirement benefits or commingle it with other money. "To maintain eligibility for paid health benefits, you have to have some money either in the Texas Teacher's Retirement System," says Briaud, or with an approved investment carrier. Check out your employer's requirements.

KNOW YOUR PENSION RIGHTS

IF YOU ARE SCHEDULED to receive a monthly pension from your employer for the rest of your life, your fortunes remain forever linked. But thanks to retirement laws that have been in place for several decades, your retirement income is protected in ways that you should understand.

IF YOUR RETIREMENT PLAN IS TERMINATED

A RETIREE'S WORST FEAR is that his or her former employer will go bankrupt and not have sufficient assets to continue to make good on its retirement obligations. To prevent retirees from having to worry about, or shoulder, such an eventuality, Congress established the Pension Benefit Guaranty Corporation (PBGC) as part of its 1974 landmark retirement legislation. Private-sector sponsors of defined benefit plans are required to pay annual premiums to purchase insurance for the benefits they have promised. Your individual pension benefit is guaranteed up to $2,642 a month, an amount that is adjusted upward for inflation.

Federal law limits the amount that you may receive from a defined benefit plan to the lower of $130,000 (the amount in 1999; it moves higher with inflation) or 100 percent of your average annual pay during your three highest-paid consecutive years of employment. If you are at the higher end of the scale, you may find the PBGC's guaranteed amount more discomfiting than consoling.

How many plans end up in the hands of the PBGC? According to statistics compiled by the Employee Benefit Research Institute, 463 plans were turned over to the agency from 1989 to 1995, about half the number that had experienced losses during the previous five-year period. As you might expect, the lower number occurred during a strong economy and the higher figure during weaker economic times.

Not all defined benefit plans are covered by the PBGC. Notable exceptions are plans established and maintained by government units or their agencies (well, let's hope *they* don't go belly up!) and plans offered by churches, fraternal associations, or professional service groups (i.e., medical, legal, or accounting practices) with fewer than twenty-five employees.

Bankruptcy or some other form of financial insolvency is not the only reason that a plan terminates. Your employer could terminate its plan because it has merged with another company or because it wants to close down one plan and start up another. If that's the case, and if your plan has sufficient assets to continue to make good on its obligations, you will be notified of the plan's termination and how the final distribution of plan assets will take place. Generally speaking, it means that you can expect your monthly stream of income to become a lump-sum distribution in short order.

IF YOUR RETIREMENT PLAN IS CHANGED

COMPANIES CHANGE THEIR names and logos; government units change their jurisdictions. It stands to reason that, over time, an employer is bound to find something to change in the pension plan it offers. However, the IRS takes a firm stand on the protections offered to individuals who are current participants in or collecting benefits from a defined benefit pension plan. Your employer can't eliminate or reduce the pension benefits that you have accrued and can't withdraw the offer of early retirement benefits or retirement-type subsidies or optional forms of benefits, such as your menu of distribution options, unless a comparable benefit, subsidy, or option is provided. In short, your employer can't amend its way out of its obligations to its existing or retired employees, and it won't find it easy to get around these rules. In fact, even if you leave your employer and return to service, paying back any distribution you received, your employer is obliged to reinstate you with the same set of benefits you had when you left—even if the firm's pension plan has been amended in the meantime. Something to keep in mind if you retire, then have second thoughts about your decision.

Today the issue of amended benefits is most likely to come up as the result of a company's merger or spinoff. And guess what? The rules still apply. Let's say that you work for American Widget, and its plan offers you the option of receiving your retirement income in annual installments over ten or twenty years. Then the company merges with International Gadget, whose plan provides for distribution in annual installments over your life expectancy. The newly combined organization has to maintain both options for employees of either company who had accrued benefits up to the time of the merger.

IF YOU CONTINUE TO WORK
AFTER NORMAL RETIREMENT AGE

GENERALLY SPEAKING, pension plans don't distribute retirement benefits until you retire. (Death and disability will also trigger benefits.) But unless your employer's pension plan has been written to exclude this option, it's possible to interpret the laws as they are currently written to allow you to work beyond normal retirement age and begin to receive retirement benefits from your employer's pension plan as if you had retired at normal retirement age—and, in fact, continue to earn additional benefits in the plan while you continue working.

If your plan happens to be one of these rare birds, and if you're the kind of person who is likely to work beyond normal retirement age anyway, are you better off taking your benefits now or suspending them? Take them, says Tom Hohl, an attorney and vice president at Fidelity Institutional Retirement Services Company. It's money in your pocket. You're entitled to the same tax options as you would have been if you had retired. That means that if you take a lump-sum distribution you may be eligible for special forward averaging. In addition, you continue to accrue benefits—although the law allows for some fancy actuarial footwork that lets your employer offset any future benefit accruals with the actuarial equivalent of the benefits you've been paid.

In reality, most plans suspend benefits for those who work beyond normal retirement age, and few plans allow you to collect while you work. But you should find out. And you should find out exactly what *does* happen to your benefits if you're determined to keep punching the time clock. Your employer can't reduce the rate at which you accrue benefits just because you're older. However, it can limit the number of years of service that count toward retirement—but that must be written into the plan.

FROM PIPELINE TO BUCKET: SOME FINAL THOUGHTS

OF ALL THE DECISIONS you will have to make about your pension, perhaps the biggest is whether to take a lump-sum distribution or a lifetime annuity, if you are offered both choices. Jim Budros, a fee-only financial planner and principal at Budros & Ruhlin in Columbus, Ohio, says that a lump-sum distribution may be financially more attractive, but it could be a psychological disaster, depending on the individual. Budros points out that the transition from being what he calls a "pipeline" person—i.e., your income is paid to you regularly—to being a "bucket" person—i.e., you have to dip into the lump sum and decide how and when to spend it—is more difficult than some people think it will be. Budros often advises people who opt for the lump sum to buy an annuity with half of it, "as a hedge against inexperience."

If you've never had an investment portfolio to manage, you should probably think twice about taking a lump-sum distribution. Theoretically, you may be able to earn a higher return for yourself. But you'll also have to deal with your emotions when the financial markets move against you. There's something to be said for knowing that your pension check will arrive every month as long as you are alive.

Once you've decided how to take your pension benefit, it's a good idea to give yourself a year to count down to retirement. It will take that long to prepare your pension game plan, and the interval should ensure enough time to process paperwork so that your benefits will be ready when you are. During the year, here are the action steps you should take:

1 Talk to your human resources contact, who may send you next to your benefits office or to an outsourcing company that has been engaged to work with you through the exit process.

2 Have a financial professional—your accountant or financial adviser—review the benefits figures you

receive. Discuss your options. Be frank about what you know—and what you don't understand—about your pension.

3 Understand the tax implications of your options.

4 Understand the potential impact of working beyond normal retirement age.

5 Make sure all the details are in place: your beneficiaries, for example, and written spousal consent if you are going to elect a single-life annuity.

Finally, call your travel agent! Well, that's what I would do. But it's optional.

CHAPTER 7

It's Your Nickel!
Your Workplace
RETIREMENT
SAVINGS PLANS

ILLIONS OF working Americans are heading for a retirement that will put them in charge of the single largest amount of money that they have ever laid their hands on. You may have started small, like Lance, my computer consultant, who was proud of—and reluctant to part with—his modest 401(k) contributions at the age of 23. But if you've been contributing the maximum to a 401(k) since the early 1980s, when they were first introduced, and you've invested in both the stock and bond markets during this roaring bull market, you could easily have half a million dollars in your 401(k) today. Certainly, most people who take advantage of these plans to the fullest can expect to retire with six- or even seven-figure accounts.

Other plans have delivered mixed results. For example, despite Polaroid's generous annual contribution of company stock equal to 5 percent of each employee's salary to its employee stock ownership plan (ESOP), a declining stock price has actually diminished the value of the savings of my ex-husband, a twenty-three-year Polaroid veteran. Then there are the loyal workers of companies such as McDonald's, Coca-Cola, and Merck, who have watched their investments in company stock go up threefold, fivefold, even tenfold since the early 1990s. Serious dollars. Serious planning requirements ahead.

In some sense, the decisions you face and the choices you will make about your savings in your defined contribution plan accounts are easier than those affecting defined benefit plan participants. For starters, the money you've accumulated is in a separate account in your name. Your employer is responsible for record keeping and accounting, for making sure your contributions are made on a timely basis, and for ensuring that your account performance is

reported to you each year, although most employers provide reports each quarter. Over the years, your employer
has offered you a menu of investment options. But you
have been responsible for the investment decisions, and
now you will be accountable for the distribution decisions
and for many of the administrative decisions involving your
defined contribution plan accounts. There are pitfalls—
and possibilities.

Before you think about how your retirement savings
plans fit into your retirement income scheme, take a few
minutes to understand something about the plans themselves. You don't need to know a lot of details. You'll find
a review of the standard withdrawal rules in Chapter 4.
Here's a quick rundown of some of the more common
defined contribution plan types with an explanation of
how withdrawals differ—if they differ—from the norm.
To make it easier to spot the exceptions, they are identified with a ✗.

If you don't recognize your plan in these descriptions,
be sure to contact your benefits office for help. Sometimes
companies give their plans cute names—American Widget's
Save-o-Matic Plan, for example. Often a company uses an
umbrella name to describe a program that includes more
than one type of plan. Polaroid's Retirement Savings Plan,
for example, comprises an ESOP, a profit-sharing plan, a
thrift plan, and a 401(k) plus the company's cash-balance
defined benefit plan. But if you're part of a qualified plan,
it should match up with one of these descriptions:

Profit-sharing plans are an employer's way of sharing its
success with its employees. Your employer's plan probably
uses a formula to determine how much it allocates to
profit-sharing accounts each year. It can allocate money to
these accounts even if it doesn't make a profit. In fact, it
can offer a profit-sharing plan even if it's a nonprofit organization, such as a university or a nonprofit hospital. But if
it's going to retain its tax-advantaged status it pretty much
has to keep up its contributions. Contributions can't be an
occasional thing.

Over the years, you may have also made voluntary contributions to your employer's profit-sharing plan. And maybe you were allowed to decide how to invest the money in the plan, choosing from a menu of investment options, which may include company stock. Fidelity Investments, for example, lets employees invest their annual profit-sharing allocations in Fidelity funds, load-free. That's been a tremendous benefit for employees astute enough to invest in funds managed by veteran Fidelity manager George Vanderheiden, whose long-term track record rivals that of former colleague Peter Lynch. On their own, investors have to fork over a sales charge ranging from 4.5 percent to 8.5 percent to get access to a fund managed exclusively by Vanderheiden.

One more feature of some profit-sharing plans: You may be able to withdraw money from your plan after you've participated for two years—even if you're still on the job. The catch is that your withdrawal is subject to a 10 percent early withdrawal penalty unless you qualify under the usual exceptions. And, of course, you'll pay income tax on the money as well.

✗ **An age-weighted plan** is a special type of profit-sharing plan which is perhaps the last place in America where an employer can legitimately discriminate on the basis of age. These plans are designed to contribute more to older participants than to younger participants. They are popular in professional offices where the staff is bifurcated between more highly compensated, older owners and senior staff members on the one hand and a lower-paid junior administrative staff on the other.

A money-purchase plan is a special type of pension plan that requires your employer to make an annual contribution. Typically contributions are calculated as a percentage of your income. You may be allowed to contribute. In fact, often when a money-purchase plan is part of a public employer's plan, you may be *required* to contribute.

When it comes time to withdraw savings from your employer's money-purchase plan, keep in mind that, as a pension plan, it must be grouped with your other pension plans in order to qualify for a lump-sum distribution. Steve Mitchell, a retirement expert and senior vice president at Fidelity Investments, says this is easily—and frequently—missed by participants and even by financial advisers.

✗ **Stock bonus plans and ESOPs** are designed to invest primarily in company stock. The difference between the two may be more apparent to your employer than to you: A plan can borrow funds to acquire employer stock for an ESOP and use the stock as collateral for the loan. ESOPs typically offer their participants the right to receive dividends in cash during their working years. You'll be taxed on these dividends, but they are one of the few benefits to pay out of a retirement savings plan without being subject to an early withdrawal penalty of 10 percent. Of course, if your employer has done well over the years, you would have been better off had you reinvested the dividends. But at least you had the choice.

There's another difference that may matter to you when you're ready to take your money: A stock bonus plan can distribute your benefit to you in cash, if you request it. However, unless there's language written into your employer's corporate charter that requires you to be an employee in order to own company stock, it must distribute your benefit to you in stock if you demand it. Often small companies that are trying to build a market for their closely held securities create stock bonus plans.

Your employer may let you cash in some or all of your ESOP after a certain period of time, while you're still working (if you do, you won't escape paying a 10 percent penalty unless you qualify under the exclusions). However, it's more common for these assets to be off limits while you're working. Perhaps that's why the IRS has the enlightened view that ESOPs should accord participants some flexibility as they count down to retirement. After all, depending on how much stock you own, how much of your retirement account it represents, and how far you are from retirement, your retirement could be enriched by your company's success or impoverished by its poor performance.

✗ Although it may put you in a difficult position if you're staring down the barrel of retirement while your firm's stock price is dead in the water, you may not have to hold on to all your company stock to the bitter end. Here's the deal: If you're at least 55 and you've worked for your employer for at least ten years, you must be allowed to diversify your ESOP holdings:

◆ Your employer must offer you a ninety-day window of opportunity to diversify at least 25 percent of your holdings. And you must be offered at least three additional investment options. Five years later, you must be allowed to diversify up to 50 percent of your holdings.

◆ Or, following the same percentage guidelines, you can actually cash in your securities and pay income tax as you go.

Generally speaking, once you retire, you'll have five years to take the stock from your employer's ESOP and roll it over into an individual retirement account (IRA), transfer it into another account, or liquidate it. In some cases, you may be able to stretch this period out—a good idea if you're trying to wait out a downturn in the value of the stock. If your stock is worth more than $500,000, you can stretch it out an additional five years.

If the stock in your ESOP isn't publicly traded, you must have the option to sell it back to your employer at a price that is arrived at through an independent appraisal. But don't count on cashing out your holdings all at once. The IRS will give your employer five years to pay for the stock in annual installments at a price you agree on up front. You'll collect interest on the outstanding amount, but chances are it won't make up for what you might have earned had you invested on your own.

If a significant portion of your retirement savings is in employer securities—in an ESOP or a stock bonus plan or a profit-sharing plan—do yourself a favor and seek professional financial advice. Do it early, and do it before you touch even one dollar or one share of stock. Missteps can be costly.

✗ **Savings or thrift plans** are designed to let you save after-tax dollars. Your employer may offer to match your savings up to a certain amount or percentage as an incentive to get you to save. Because your part of the savings comes from money on which you've already paid income tax, savings and thrift plan withdrawals are treated differently. You'll pay income tax only on contributions your employer has made and on the earnings you've accumulated over the years. But there's another difference to keep in mind when you start thinking about strategies to consolidate your tax-deferred retirement assets and the options that let you do this: You can't roll over this after-tax money with other retirement plan savings.

401(k) plan. The big one. More than 25 million workers at more than 270,000 companies participate in 401(k) plans. Over the years, you have elected to have part of your salary contributed to your plan, which may, in fact, be a profit-sharing or stock bonus plan. The money has gone into an account with your name on it. You have made the decisions on how to invest it, choosing from a menu of options offered by your employer.

In 1996 Congress enacted legislation that made it easier for small companies to offer retirement plans. One version of the Savings Incentive Match Plan for Employees or SIMPLE plan is a 401(k). If you're covered by one, you haven't been able to put in as much money as have participants in regular 401(k) plans. Why? No really good reason. But here's one thought: Unlike 401(k) plans, in which employers can get away without contributing a dime, your employer has been required to kick in between 1 and 3 percent of your income to your SIMPLE 401(k), even if you have not contributed. If the contribution limit was higher, that raises the dollar amount your employer would have to put in. I suppose that could discourage a small company from adopting the plan in the first place.

Another difference between SIMPLE 401(k)s and their big brothers: The money in your account is yours from day one: no waiting around for vesting. The theory is that turnover is higher among small companies, and you can move from one to another during your working years and roll your retirement savings over into a new employer's plan without leaving anything on the table at your previous job. SIMPLEs also target another trend: The move by many American workers to part-time employment at a small company late in their career cycle. As long as you earn $5,000, you can participate.

403(b). If you are a teacher, a preacher, a doctor, or a do-gooder, chances are you're covered by a plan similar to a 401(k) called a 403(b) plan, which may also be referred to as a tax-deferred annuity (TDA) or tax-sheltered annuity (TSA), harking back to an earlier time when the savings directed to one of these plans were required to be invested in the form of an insured annuity contract. That changed in 1974, along with other changes in the laws that govern both the money that goes into your 403(b) plan and how and when the money comes out.

In fact, today most 403(b) or TDA plans must comply with most rules that apply to qualified plans. Yet they are not qualified plans. According to a spokesperson in the Richmond, Virginia, office of William M. Mercer, Inc., the rules that apply to 403(b) plans are in some ways more complex than those that apply to qualified plans, but they are also more flexible. In general, most of the usual rules apply: The money is available to you with no strings attached after you're 59½ and generally speaking you'll have to start taking it when you're 70½ unless you're still working. Participants in 403(b) plans may be surprised to learn that the law does not require them to take their retirement money in the form of an annuity even if they've been saving through an annuity. Your right of payment will be controlled by the contract you signed, and many of these allow for lump-sum distributions. You can roll your money over; you can transfer it from one annuity to another if you don't like your annuity provider. You'll pay no income tax on such a rollover, but you will pay income tax on your withdrawals, and there are no favorable tax treatments available to you. Beyond these basic guidelines, there are some interesting quirks about taking money from your 403(b) that are worth knowing:

◆ For example, you may be able to take a withdrawal from your 403(b) before you're 59½. Here's the deal: If you were saving money in a 403(b) tax-sheltered annuity prior to 1988, when the law changed to limit access to such savings before retirement, your account balance up to that time is protected by earlier laws that said you could withdraw it before age 59½. This grandfathered provision does not apply if you invested in mutual funds. So if you are considering moving your money from an annuity to a mutual fund, recognize that you might be giving up a valuable right. In addition, if you move your money from one annuity to another, make sure the first company tells the second company of your December 31, 1988, account balance to preserve the grandfathering.

◆ In fact, if your 403(b) has been funded by your employer's contributions, not yours, and you are invested in an annuity contract and not in mutual funds, there's still no law that restricts you from taking that money out before you're 59½, although you may have to pay a 10 percent penalty. The restriction applies only to accounts that contain your contributions. However, laws aside, most employers are careful to write some restriction into their plan documents. Most employers believe that if they are setting money aside for your retirement, it should be used for that purpose. But unlike most other restrictions on retirement money, it's not a matter of the Internal Revenue Code.

◆ One of the most interesting features of a 403(b) plan actually kicks in just before you retire: If you haven't taken full advantage of your ability to contribute the maximum to your account, there's a window just before you reach normal retirement age during which you can make up for lost time. You may be able to add an additional $15,000 to your retirement account—not a bad deal if you can afford to do it. But according to Tom Peller, a Boston attorney who specializes in retirement issues, the amount each individual is entitled to add during this catch-up phase results from a complicated calculation. In some cases, your employer may help with the calculation, or refer it to an actuarial firm that specializes in such calculations. But you will need some help to get it right.

◆ One more exception: The money that you saved in a 403(b) before 1986 is not subject to standard required minimum withdrawal rules. Instead, Fidelity's Steve Mitchell says that this money is governed by old annuity rules that are generally interpreted to mean that you have to make a good-faith attempt to take at least half of it out over your lifetime. And you can postpone withdrawals until you're 75. However, only the amount of money you had in the plan before 1986 is exempt from today's standard required minimum withdrawal rules, not the earnings on it, and not anything you've added since.

Church plans. Hallelujah! There are exceptions accorded to church retirement plans that are designed to make this special class of 403(b) plans more flexible. And there's more than one definition of a *church*. For example, your employer may be exempt from some of the official rules that govern other qualified plans, but it still has to abide by nondiscrimination rules that level the savings opportunities for highly compensated and less highly compensated employees. A lot of church-run hospitals meet this definition. For example, the Adventist HealthCare organization, which employs about 41,000 individuals, may be exempt from some national laws, but it must still meet nondiscrimination rules. Bill Easterbrook, vice president of Adventist HealthCare Retirement Plans, says they adhere to all the most important rules that govern qualified plans. The plan's fiduciary oversight is impeccable; in fact, the only thing it's short on is bells and whistles, and Easterbrook and his team are working on that.

Actual churches have a lot more flexibility. They don't have to cover all their employees: I can remember being astounded that my sister wasn't included in the plan sponsored by a parochial school in which she taught years ago, but male teachers were! A church can even set up its plan to take direct charge of employee contributions, hire its own investment managers, and manage the money itself. An opportunity for abuse? It exists. If you are part of a church plan, I'd suggest you find out how your savings are handled. God is in the details.

457 plans. Many state and local governments offer plans that allow their employees to defer compensation into tax-advantaged accounts similar to 401(k)s and 403(b)s. If you are part of one of these plans, you may know it simply as the [Name of Your County] Retirement Savings Plan, but technically these are called 457 plans, after the Internal Revenue Code section that put them on the books. Often government employers combine these with traditional pension plans to help employees save a little extra to enrich their retirements.

Like 403(b)s, 457 plans are not qualified plans. They lack a level of fiduciary protection that's guaranteed by qualified plans. Until recently, their assets were vulnerable to creditors, a provision that may not seem problematic in these flush economic times. However, in the 1970s, when New York City was on the brink of bankruptcy, or more recently, when California's Orange County stumbled badly in a derivatives scandal, employees' retirement assets were fair game for creditors. Yet one good piece of legislation came out of that debacle: In 1996, Congress passed a law that requires the money set aside for employees in a governmental 457 plan to be held in trust for their exclusive benefit. That should make it harder to get at.

There are other differences: 457 plans rarely provide the same range of investment options available to 401(k) participants. And withdrawal options are more limited than with other types of plans. For example, you can't roll money saved in a 457 plan into an IRA. There are no favorable tax treatments available if you withdraw all the money in your plan at once. Your only distribution options are an annuity, assuming your account is worth at least $5,000, or a lump sum.

But there's also some good news: There is no penalty for early withdrawals from a 457 plan. As long as you're separating from service, the money is yours if you want it. (You'll be liable for income tax.)

These plans also have a catch-up provision similar to that of 403(b)s. If you haven't taken full advantage of your ability to contribute the maximum $8,000 to your account ($7,500 prior to 1998 or 33⅓ percent of your taxable income, whichever is less) each year, there's a three-year window just before you reach normal retirement age during which you may be able to add an additional $15,000 to your retirement account. The actual amount you can catch up will be the difference between what you could have put in and what you didn't put in during the years you were eligible for contributions after 1978. You're only entitled to one three-year catch-up period. And you can't use a catch-up period if you opt for early retirement, i.e., you agree to retire and receive partial benefits from your employer's plan.

Deferred-compensation plans. Companies often reward their top executives with the offer to set aside income in a special account to be tapped—and taxed—at retirement. Executive deferred-compensation plans are dicey. If you're a million-dollar-a-year executive at Microsoft you might feel pretty secure that the company will be around to deliver on its promise some years down the road. And if it's a way to remove income from the current tax year, why not take advantage of it?

But deferred-compensation plans are in a class by themselves when it comes to retirement. They aren't qualified plans. You can't do anything with the money due you but take it once you leave your employer or retire. And then there are no favorable tax treatments—all the money is taxable in the year you receive it. Unless you've made an election when you commence participation to receive your benefit as an annuity when you retire, you must take all of it at once, because the law is written to provide that when you *can* take it, you *must* take it and pay any taxes that are due. What's more, the election, if you make it, is irrevocable. And a lengthy payout period raises the risk for the participant—if your former employer goes bankrupt while you're collecting, you're out of luck.

Lisa Alkon, an attorney in the Boston office of William M. Mercer, Inc., says there is one thing you should think about if you have money due you from a deferred-compensation plan: Because it's subject to Social Security withholding, or FICA, you can save up to $4,000 by retiring late in the year, when you'll probably have already satisfied the maximum 6.2 percent withholding. Your employer will thank you, because the firm will be spared the matching tax.

Keogh Plans: different, but the same. As early as the 1960s, Congress recognized the need for individuals who were self-employed—or ran professional practices, small companies, or the family farm—to have a way to save for retirement. The first attempt to popularize retirement savings for individuals and small businesses was the Keogh Plan, which was really a mini–retirement plan that could contain inside it any number of options that might be found in a large-company plan. It could be constructed as a profit-sharing plan or even a traditional pension plan. Like other qualified plans, Keoghs involve a fair amount of paperwork, which may be the reason they have never caught on in a big way.

If you have saved money for retirement in a Keogh, your withdrawals are subject to the same rules that apply to other qualified plans (see Chapter 4, page 73). You can roll Keogh assets over into an IRA, which is not a bad idea if you—or you and your spouse—are the only participants. You can terminate the Keogh and dump the paperwork.

You're also eligible for a lump-sum distribution, and if you take it after you're 59½, you may be eligible for special tax treatment such as forward averaging. Otherwise, you'll pay ordinary income tax on your withdrawals as you receive them.

CHAPTER

On Your Own:
Your Individual
RETIREMENT
SAVINGS

A S COMPLICATED AS MOST workplace retirement savings plans are, the ones that were designed primarily for individual savings get the prize: Is there a law that says that IRAs *have* to change every year? The good news, however, is that despite the numerous tax law changes that affect contributions to individual retirement savings plans, the rules that govern withdrawals have changed very little. In general, it's pretty simple to turn these accounts into income. With the Roth IRA, it's easy because withdrawals are tax-free if you play by the rules. But the rules that govern withdrawals from individual savings are different from those that apply to your workplace pension or retirement savings plans, and generally speaking, they're less flexible.

INDIVIDUAL RETIREMENT ACCOUNTS

In 1974, Congress introduced Individual Retirement Accounts (IRAs) to give workers who weren't covered by an employer's retirement plan the opportunity to save on their own and provide a tax incentive to make saving attractive. You could deduct your contributions from your income tax, receive tax-deferred earnings that could compound until you took the money out, and do it all with a $1,500 annual contribution limit that was a realistic target for average Americans, especially when you factored in the immediate income tax savings. In the twenty-five years since they first showed up in the vocabulary of working Americans, IRAs have undergone some change with virtually every new tax law. The biggest changes were to raise the contribution limit to $2,000, to extend greater saving power to nonworking spouses, and to, restrict their tax deductibility for most workers covered by other plans. However, even without the offer of an immediate tax break, IRAs have become the mainstay retirement savings option for many Americans. They have also given rise to a number of variations. A special IRA account called a **ROLLOVER IRA** or **CONDUIT IRA** makes an attractive parking place for money you've saved in an employer's retirement plan. If you leave the company, or retire and don't need the money, you can roll your savings over into an IRA and keep them accumulating tax-deferred earnings until you withdraw them.

Financial experts believe that most of us will accumulate money in a rollover IRA at some point or another during our working lives, as we are moving from job to job, or at retirement, when we are ready to create a plan for turning our savings into income.

IRAs EXPANDED

IN 1978, CONGRESS extended the IRA concept to employers, who could offer a **SIMPLIFIED EMPLOYEE PENSION PLAN** (also known as a **SEP IRA** because it allowed employers to make contributions to IRAs on behalf of employees and for themselves) as an alternative to a qualified retirement plan, with all its paperwork and associated legal costs. Contribution limits are in line with the total benefits limit for qualified plans. A special type of SEP called a **SALARY REDUCTION SIMPLIFIED EMPLOYEE PENSION PLAN (SARSEP),** which resembles a 401(k), allows employees to defer part of their compensation into a retirement plan along with employer contributions. But these were superseded by the **SAVINGS INCENTIVE MATCH PLAN FOR EMPLOYEES** or **SIMPLE PLAN** in 1996. Your employer's SIMPLE plan may be a 401(k) or an IRA. And depending which one your employer offers, it will operate under slightly different rules.

Withdrawals from SIMPLE 401(k)s generally follow rules that apply to 401(k)s. SIMPLE IRAs are different in one key respect: The penalty for withdrawing money from a SIMPLE IRA any time during the first two years you're covered by it is a whopping 25 percent, regardless of age or circumstance. You can't roll your savings over into an IRA that is not a SIMPLE IRA if you leave the company. In fact, if you do you're asking for trouble: Not only are you liable for the penalty, but the money you roll over is treated like an ordinary IRA contribution. And if it's more than the $2,000 annual IRA limit, now you've got an excess contribution—and it's subject to a 6 percent penalty every year until you get it out!

In 1996, Congress unveiled the most tempting IRA ever. The **ROTH IRA** makes it possible to save up to $2,000 a year for retirement with the promise of tax-free withdrawals forever. If you've been saving for retirement in an IRA, or if you've rolled retirement plan assets over into an IRA, you have the option of paying your taxes now and converting to a Roth IRA to ensure future tax-free withdrawals. You have to meet income eligibility requirements and your assets have to stay put for five years before withdrawals. Deciding whether it makes sense to convert takes more than a few scratches on the back of an envelope. See Chapters 5 and 11, and talk to a financial adviser. There's also an excellent Web site devoted exclusively to Roth IRAs. Find it at www.rothira.com.

TAKING MONEY FROM YOUR INDIVIDUAL RETIREMENT ACCOUNTS

ROTH IRAS PUT the decision about taking your money squarely into your hands. After all, you've paid your taxes. After five years, all the money is yours to take tax- and penalty-free. So the IRS doesn't really care whether you take a lot or a little, now or later. Some financial experts say that it's only a matter of time until they *will* care about Roth IRA assets that are left to grow as part of an individual's estate for the purpose of transferring tax-free wealth to the next generation. But for now, if a Roth makes sense for all the other reasons, you're off the hook as to how and when you take your money.

The rules that govern withdrawals from traditional IRAs, including rollover IRAs and SEPs, are not that attractive, and they are in fact generally less flexible than those that apply to workplace retirement savings plans. For example, there's no automatic penalty-free access at 55 if you're separated from your job, as there is with a qualified plan. And there's no getting around required minimum distributions once you're 70½. Unlike workplace savings plans that were recently changed to let you push out withdrawals as long as you are still working (and as long as you don't own at least 5 percent of the company for which you work), 70½ is it. No more contributions; it's time to take the money. If you have multiple IRA accounts, you can choose to take minimum distributions from each one, or use one account to satisfy the withdrawal requirements. But you've got to start taking the money and paying income tax on it.

In addition, there is no favorable tax treatment for money that you take out of an IRA. It's taxed as ordinary income, and that's it. If you've rolled money over into an IRA, you've given up your right to forward averaging. And in some states money in an IRA is exposed to creditors' claims, which is not the case for money left in a qualified retirement plan.

When you begin taking money out of your IRAs, you'll pay tax on all of the money you withdraw from deductible IRAs, but only part of your withdrawals from your non-deductible IRAs are taxable—the portion that can be attributed to your investment earnings. The IRS provides a formula for this calculation (see Chapter 4), which requires that you've kept good enough records to establish how much money you contributed over the years to your nondeductible IRAs. Don't cop out on the paperwork and the calculation—otherwise you'll be paying income tax twice on your retirement savings.

One more thing about IRAs and SEPs: It's harder to get around the 10 percent early withdrawal penalty. The exceptions are death, disability, certain medical expenses, and substantially equal periodic payments for life. You can also get around it if you take money out to purchase your first home or to pay educational costs. But few people are in that boat as they enter retirement. Clearly these accounts were meant for retirement, and the penalty should make you think twice before you use this money for any other purpose.

TURNING
Your Assets into Income

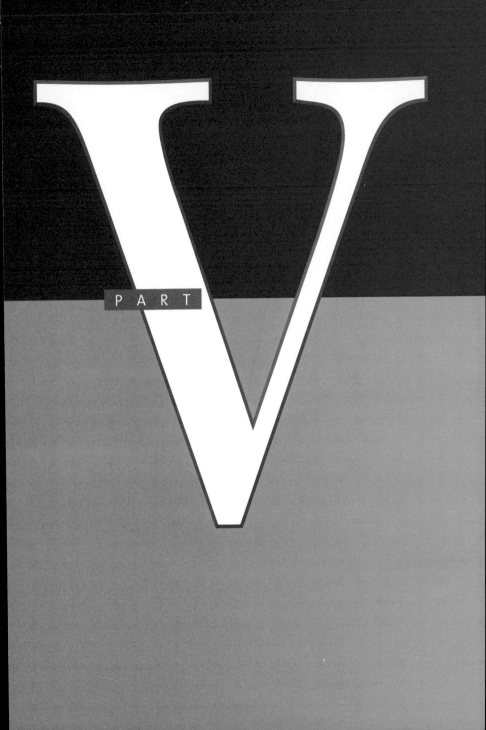

PART

V

CHAPTER

9

CREATING
YOUR
Retirement
Paycheck

HO WILL sign the checks for your retirement income? Social Security, probably. Your former employer's pension plan, maybe. If you're like my folks, who collect federal and state government pensions, you may expect nothing more from your savings than supplemental income—in other words, money you could live without but will be happy you don't have to. If that's your situation, you need a plan to make it easy to get at your savings and an idea of how much you can take out each year.

If you're like me, however, and you expect your retirement savings to play a major role in covering your monthly living expenses, you're in charge of creating your own retirement paycheck. And you'll need a tactical plan to make sure the income is there as long as you need it. Sure, I'm counting on Social Security. Lot's of people laugh at it, but as meager as it is, I figure it will make my mortgage payments. What's so bad about that?

But it's my 401(k) and profit-sharing plan from a former employer, plus the SEP IRA I've maintained during the years that I've run my own business, that will have to pay most of the bills. Like many baby boomers, I don't see early retirement as an option. I'm still paying college tuition, and I don't expect to be able to put down my pen at 65, the age my mom was when she retired. But even if I work until I'm 70, I have to plan for a twenty-year retirement.

The 1990s bull market has also produced a new retirement phenomenon: Thousands of American workers for whom early retirement is a very real alternative. If you linked your fate to a small, growing company, you may find yourself in your 30s, 40s, or 50s with a bonanza in appreciated company stock, thanks to a successful public offering. Or, if you work for a large, blue-chip company, a run-up in your employer's stock price may have enriched the value of your retirement plan so that you're asking yourself: Why am I still working?

However, it's important to map out your retirement income; what seems like a mountain of money today may not support you into your 80s or 90s. Besides, early retirement is more than a financial decision. "Few people can do nothing and really enjoy it," says Judith Shine, president of Denver-based Shine Investment Advisory Services, Inc. Instead of retirement, Shine advises clients to consider doing something different, "something they really like—and less of it."

Finally, if you are a woman, planning your retirement paycheck takes special care. Your life expectancy is longer than a man's by about seven years, all other things being equal. And although women have made great strides in the workplace, there is an incredible gender gap that shows up during retirement. According to the Employee Benefit Research Institute, the income differential between men and women aged 65+ is high—around 40 percent. For women aged 55–64, however, the gap is even higher—around 60 percent, and it has risen slightly in the 1990s while the gap for older women has come down slightly.

REAL MEDIAN INCOME, IN 1994 DOLLARS, BY GENDER

YEAR	MALES		FEMALES		DIFFERENCE %	
	55–64	65+	55–64	65+	55–64	65+
1955	$6,750	$6,100	$6,400	$3,600	5	41
1960	$19,740	$7,815	$6,515	$3,780	67	52
1965	$24,210	$9,100	$8,750	$4,265	64	53
1970	$27,550	$11,040	$10,570	$5,460	62	51
1975	$28,060	$13,075	$10,285	$7,120	63	46
1980	$28,660	$12,215	$8,870	$7,610	69	38
1985	$27,900	$15,015	$9,880	$8,695	65	42
1990	$28,125	$16,080	$10,660	$9,120	62	43
1992	$25,057	$15,420	$10,700	$8,645	57	44
1994	$27,075	$15,250	$10,870	$8,950	60	41

SOURCE: EMPLOYEE BENEFIT RESEARCH INSTITUTE, 1998

IF YOUR SAVINGS
PROVIDE THE EXTRAS

IF YOU COUNT YOURSELF among the millions of Americans who expect Social Security and your employer's monthly pension payment to provide enough income to live on each month, your strategy should be to:

◆ Tap your taxable savings first, for the extras and special purchases.

◆ Take as little as you can from your tax-deferred retirement savings until you're required to take minimum distributions. Then give special attention to minimum required distribution options that will allow you to stretch out your withdrawals as long as possible (see Chapter 10).

◆ Keep an eye on your total annual income. Don't let the money you withdraw from a tax-deferred account, on which you'll pay income tax, push you into a new tax bracket unnecessarily.

◆ If you continue to work part time, consider putting money into a Roth IRA as a legacy for your heirs.

If you expect to use your savings to travel or to augment your holiday gift budget, put yourself on an allowance and create a separate account for it. That will make your expenditures easier and will enforce a discipline to keep you from overspending. For example, Don and Carol Hollingsworth, a Massachusetts couple in their 60s, have a cache of savings bonds and a modest IRA account that Carol accumulated over the years to supplement Don's pension from a private university and their combined Social Security benefits.

Every year in January, the couple cashes in 5 percent of their savings bonds and puts the money into a money market mutual fund, where it continues to earn a market rate of interest. "That's our extra spending money for the year," says Carol. Because they can write checks on their money market fund, they can use it whenever and however they want. Anything that remains in the account at the end of the year, the couple uses to buy additional bonds.

When Carol turns 70½, she will have to begin minimum withdrawals from her IRA. Then, they'll reassess their annual supplemental income needs. "We may be able to leave the savings bonds to our grandchildren," says Carol. But in the meantime, her IRA keeps growing tax-deferred. If it averages a 10 percent return, she'll have doubled her money by the time she is required to begin withdrawals.

GIVE YOURSELF A RAISE

IF YOU'RE USING YOUR savings to supplement your income so that you can enjoy a few extras, be sure to give yourself a raise now and then in recognition of the fact that inflation eats away at your purchasing power to the tune of about 3.5 percent a year over the long term. Recently, it's been less than 2 percent. However, if inflation reverts to its historical norm, the value of your current spending will lose half its purchasing power in twenty years. That's sobering when you consider that you'll also be twenty years older, and not in a strong position to go out and add to your savings.

But then think how your lifestyle will change over the next twenty years. Judith Shine feels that most retirees fail to consider that they will live very differently in their 70s and 80s than they did in their 50s and 60s. "You don't buy the latest fashion or redecorate your home when you're in your 70s and 80s," says Shine. If you're weighing your concern for the future against the pleasure of having some of the extras that can make your life rewarding today, Shine comes down on the side of living for today, especially when you're talking about discretionary funds.

LIVE ON A PENSION—LIVE IT UP ON YOUR SAVINGS

◆ Direct Social Security and pension checks to your checking account.
◆ Allot an annual amount from taxable savings and direct it to a money market account with check-writing privileges.
◆ Preserve your tax-deferred savings until you're 70½ or as a resource of last resort.

IF YOUR SAVINGS PAY THE BILLS

IF YOU EXPECT THE NEST EGG you've accumulated to generate income that you'll need to meet your monthly bills—whether it's 20 percent or 100 percent of them— your challenges are:

◆ To be realistic about the amount of money you withdraw each month so that there's income when you need it ten, twenty, or even thirty years down the road.

◆ To make payday a convenient process.

Before you can do either, ask yourself what role you want to play in creating your retirement income.

FROM REALITY CHECK TO PAYCHECK

BEFORE YOU CALL YOUR benefits office and ask for a lump-sum distribution from your pension plan or set up a rollover account for your 401(k) savings, before you start figuring whether you can withdraw 5 percent or 8 percent of your assets each year, ask yourself these questions: Can you handle this process on your own? And do you want to? Would you feel more comfortable turning it over to a professional manager, who will decide how to turn your assets into income? Do you want to know that a check in the same amount is in the mail every month, and be done with it? Do you like the challenge of getting the most from your savings—and are you comfortable with the risks associated with becoming the chairman of the board of Your Retirement, Inc.?

Be honest with yourself about the amount of time you want to spend, about your comfort with the financial markets, and about your ability to stick to a strategy without buckling when the markets get volatile. Remember, if you stay flexible, you can change your mind down the road.

WHAT'S YOUR INCOME PROFILE?

ALTHOUGH EACH ONE of us has a unique set of circumstances—different family health patterns, different reactions to market volatility, different approaches to responsibility,

and varying levels of knowledge about the financial markets—most people fall into one of three categories:

◆ **THE INCOME DELEGATOR** is happy to turn the responsibility
for creating his or her retirement paycheck over to
someone else. If you are a delegator, you may hire a
financial adviser or a professional money manager, go
to a financial services firm or bank that offers discretionary money management services, or choose an asset
allocation or balanced mutual fund that offers a systematic withdrawal option.

◆ **THE INCOME WORRIER** is afraid of one thing—a minus
sign—and needs an income solution that comes with
promises and guarantees. If you are an income worrier,
you may buy a fixed-income annuity with your taxable
savings; you may convert your retirement savings account
into an income annuity; or you may create a conservative
portfolio of bonds, certificates of deposit, and other
short-term investments that will preserve your capital and
generate a relatively predictable income stream.

◆ **THE INCOME MANAGER** is both interested in and confident
about taking on the challenge of creating a retirement
paycheck. If you are a manager, as my son says, "You da
Man." You'll be responsible for creating and managing
your portfolio to generate the income you need at a
level of risk that feels comfortable. You'll also be responsible for the mechanics of paying yourself monthly or
quarterly—or at some other interval that meets your
needs.

You may begin your retirement in one category and end
up in another. Some delegators get frustrated and decide
to try their hands as managers. On the other hand, many
a manager grows into a delegator over time. It can be a
full-time job to stay on top of your investments, handle the
paperwork, and keep the money flowing into your income
account.

Some worriers are delegators, but not all. There are
plenty of manager/worriers who are unlikely ever to
become delegators (my dad, for example). Delegators who

have had a bad experience sometimes end up as worriers, for better or for worse. If your professional investment manager loses 10 percent when the market is off 20 percent and you bail out, it's probably a bad move—but then, you were probably a worrier all along. And managers can end up as worriers if they discover they're in over their heads.

You get the gist. Now where do you see yourself in the following profiles?

THE INCOME DELEGATOR

IF YOU HAVE AT LEAST $200,000 in retirement savings and you want to delegate the responsibility for turning it into income to a professional, you'll find plenty of offers of help. Most major investment companies offer such services, but the fees can vary widely. Fidelity's Portfolio Advisory Services, for example, charges using a sliding scale starting at 1.0 percent and falling to 0.5 percent, in addition to fund management fees, to create a portfolio of mutual funds that matches your financial profile and income goals. They waive any fund loads, so it can be a pretty good deal.

With the same amount of money, American Express Financial Advisors will select a tailored portfolio of individual stocks and bonds that matches your goals. You'll have the advantage of one-on-one access to a dedicated financial professional. However, you could pay a higher fee for the service—fees range from 0.5 percent to 3.0 percent, a matter to be negotiated with your financial adviser.

Professional management is just one benefit of these services. When the markets go a little haywire, you won't have your finger on the trigger with your retirement at stake. That can be important if you are investing a lump-sum distribution from your plan. If professional management keeps you from making one bad call because you've gotten cold feet on your investment strategy, it's probably worth the money you pay for it and then some. Bottom line: Know yourself, and choose a course of action that plays to your strengths and covers your weaknesses.

Unlike the big financial service firms, most independent

money management firms (those run by individuals or small groups) are primarily interested in accounts of $1 million or more—which is not to say that you can't get their attention for less. But if you do, chances are they'll invest your money in mutual funds because the economies of scale for an individually managed portfolio just aren't there. The fee you'll pay to have someone like Jim Budros, a fee-only financial planner and principal at Budros & Ruhlin, of Columbus, Ohio, put together your retirement portfolio and manage it for you is closer to what you'll pay Fidelity. The advantage, even if you end up in mutual funds, is that you should get access to more investment choices and more personalized service.

There's no minimum account size required at Lowell, Blake & Associates in Boston. Investors pay a flat annual fee for service each year, because that's the way President Jim Lowell thinks his business ought to work. Chat Reynders, a Lowell, Blake vice president, says that fee ends up being less than 0.5 percent of assets under management for most of their clients.

You can't be a dyed-in-the-wool delegator if you work with Lowell, Blake. They don't typically take discretionary control of client assets. Clients are required to be part of all decisions. And Jim Lowell reserves the right to resign from your account if he doesn't think you're holding up your end of the bargain.

Most advisers will meet several times with a first-time client to assess priorities before initiating an income plan. Here are some typical questions:

◆ **HOW MUCH MONTHLY INCOME DO YOU NEED?** And you were probably wondering how much income you could *get!* Your answer will help your adviser create a withdrawal strategy. If your income expectations are high relative to your assets, you will probably have to make a choice: a more aggressive investment strategy, drawing your principal down to zero within your lifetime, or lowering your income expectations. If your expectations are low, your adviser will want to discuss estate planning strategies for assets that remain in your retirement accounts after you're gone.

◆ **IS IT MORE IMPORTANT TO MAXIMIZE YOUR INCOME OR PRESERVE YOUR ASSETS TO CREATE AN ESTATE FOR YOUR HEIRS?** The answer will help your adviser determine both an investment strategy and a withdrawal strategy.

◆ **HOW DO YOU WANT YOUR RETIREMENT INCOME PAID TO YOU?** The precise mechanics of your income plan are important. If you travel regularly or maintain more than one residence, it's usually better to set up a separate income account and have your monthly check deposited for you than to have a check cut from your accounts and mailed to you along with your statement.

Dee Lee, a certified financial planner in Harvard, Massachusetts, likes to ladder a bond portfolio (i.e., hold bonds of varying maturities, from short to long, so that some mature every year or two) to generate a predictable income stream, which is deposited in a client's account. The mechanics make sense—although many advisers believe it can be a mistake to think of your retirement income and your investment income as one and the same.

You don't have to have $200,000 to delegate your retirement paycheck to a professional manager. In fact, you can usually get access to so-called wrap accounts—discre-

---

DO YOUR HOMEWORK BEFORE YOU DELEGATE

◆ **IF YOU HAVE LESS THAN $200,000** consider an asset allocation or balanced mutual fund and a systematic withdrawal from your employer's plan.

◆ **IF YOU HAVE BETWEEN $200,000 AND $500,000** choose an investment firm that offers tailored portfolios, good service, and low fees.

◆ **IF YOU HAVE AT LEAST $500,000** consider a personal investment adviser. Ask about credentials, track record, and fees.

tionary management wrapped around individual mutual funds—with as little as $50,000. However, the fees on such accounts are typically high and the benefits are debatable. If that's your situation, chances are you'll be better off if you choose an income-oriented asset allocation fund or balanced mutual fund, target a withdrawal rate, and arrange for systematic withdrawals into an account that you'll use for your regular income. However, you'll end up with most of the headaches of an income manager, including the one that is bound to show up when the financial markets turn volatile and you're wondering whether you should stick with your strategy.

THE INCOME WORRIER

IF YOU DON'T SEE YOURSELF as an investor, comfortable with the risks associated with the ups and downs of the financial market—remember, there's no guarantee that a professional money manager will generate the income you desire—you may opt to roll your retirement assets into a fixed-income annuity. That's certainly the most conservative choice you can make, the easiest choice—and also the most permanent choice.

You could divide your annuity between fixed and variable accounts, but if you're really looking for freedom from financial decisions—and a guarantee—a fixed-income annuity may be best for you, even if you forfeit future flexibility and growth potential. It's easy for someone to tell you that you could make more money by investing on your own. But it's more important to follow your instincts.

Don't be swayed by the financial press's generally sour attitude toward income annuities, which I think you can chalk up to both their youth and the general inability of someone who is pretty smart with numbers to see the non-financial aspect of something as personal as money. The financial markets have been so robust it's hard for them to understand why anyone would settle for a 5 percent return, and it's equally hard for a savvy, well-educated 28-year-old reporter to comprehend that there are worse things than having to reduce your retirement income expectations.

One of the strongest objections to annuities today is that interest rates are so low that if you buy a fixed lifetime annuity, your dollars will purchase far less income than you could have gotten even six or seven years ago. That's true: In 1990, a $100,000 annuity would have purchased lifetime income of $900 a month for a 65-year-old male. Today the same $100,000 will buy $690 a month.

There are no easy alternatives. You might consider delaying retirement. But that's no help if you really do need an income plan that works today. You could put the money into the stock market, waiting for bond yields to rise. But when that happens, it's likely that it will be driven by a declining stock market. Higher bond yields will mean you get more income per annuity dollar—but if you've lost money in the stock market, you'll have less money than you started out with to buy your annuity. There's no free lunch.

If a guaranteed stream of income suits your needs, shop wisely. Choose an insurance company with a good rating, an established track record, and low fees. Don't believe for a moment that all annuities are the same. Pay a visit to the Annuity Shopper Web site (www.annuityshopper.com), which shows payouts from dozens of companies. For more information about annuities, including variable annuity options, see Chapter 5.

There are alternatives to an income annuity that may satisfy the worrier in you if you are knowledgeable about the financial markets and you don't mind doing some of the work. You can structure a portfolio of high-quality bonds that may do as well as or better than an annuity. And if you discipline yourself to live on your income—or set a fixed percentage withdrawal rate—you should have something to pass on to your heirs, something that's possible to structure with an income annuity—but not without sacrificing the amount of income you'll receive during your lifetime.

If you go the bond portfolio route, it's also important to keep your costs low. If you buy U.S. Treasury bonds from your bank or brokerage, you may pay $40 to $50 per transaction. However, if you buy the same bonds directly from the Federal Reserve Bank, which you can do by establishing an account through its TreasuryDirect program, you'll eliminate all transaction costs.

You also need an account with a commercial bank or brokerage so that the Fed can wire interest payments and matured principal on any bonds you buy. For more information about the Fed's TreasuryDirect program, including information about opening and maintaining a TreasuryDirect account, check out the Treasury Web site at www.publicdebt.treas.gov. In fact, once you open an account, you can buy Treasury securities over the phone or on-line.

Why not use a bond mutual fund to generate your retirement income? I won't go so far as to say never invest in a bond fund. However, if you're really a worrier, you could be disappointed in their volatility. In 1994, when the world's bond markets suffered one of their worst collective losses ever, bond fund investors lost principal. That's because funds have to price their securities to market each day. However, if you owned long-term U.S. Treasury bonds, which gave up more than 10 percent of their value in 1994, what did you care? You didn't lose anything. You received income on schedule. And if you felt a little flush the next year, when long-term Treasury values skyrocketed more than 35 percent, maybe you sold a few, bought some more—and pocketed your gains (after taxes, of course).

THE INCOME MANAGER

IF YOU DECIDE TO TAKE charge of your own retirement paycheck, you have your work cut out for you. On the one hand, it will give you a chance to get the very most out of your retirement dollars. On the other, it's a big responsibility. You need a plan of action. And you need to give yourself about six months' lead time. Why so long? Because your plan will almost invariably include moving accounts from one institution to another—a process that can be fraught with human error.

STEP ONE: CONSOLIDATE

YOUR GOAL IS TO consolidate the money from all your

retirement savings plans into the fewest possible accounts and relationships that can still deliver:

◆ Flexibility and variety to keep your investments working hard.

◆ Convenience to make payday easy.

So what does that mean? One account? Six accounts? That depends on whether you have more than one kind of retirement plan and/or IRA, and whether your aim is to keep required minimum withdrawals easy when you're 70½ or you have other priorities.

Start with your individual retirement savings. For tax purposes, it's easier if you separate deductible from nondeductible IRAs. Then, unless you have estate planning reasons not to, consolidate your traditional IRAs into two accounts. If you have a Roth IRA, you'll have to keep it separate from other IRAs. If your IRA accounts are at different financial institutions, bring them under one roof. Is that risky? A variation on putting all your eggs in one basket? Not if it's a big financial supermarket like Fidelity, Merrill Lynch, or Charles Schwab. These are solid companies with public records of success. Some of the nation's largest banks are working hard to build similar networks and offerings, but I don't think they are there yet. However, if your portfolio is simple, and you value a strong, personal, and local relationship, check out what your bank can offer.

Consolidate workplace retirement savings. The easiest way is to roll everything over into a single rollover IRA. It's practical. If you don't consolidate, you'll be required to take minimum withdrawals from each plan when you reach 70½. You can't aggregate them. And Denver investment adviser Judith Shine thinks that it's also psychologically easier for most people to deal with one big investment position than with lots of scattered resources.

If you have IRAs that you've used for saving $2,000 each year, can you roll your workplace savings into one of these? You can, but you probably shouldn't. It may be a long shot, but if you change your mind about retirement and go back to work, you won't be able to roll the money from your workplace savings plan into your new employer's retirement plan if you've commingled it with other IRA money. That's not the worst thing, but in general anything that reduces your flexibility regarding your retirement money is worth avoiding if you can do so.

Some money can't be rolled over—money in a deferred-compensation plan, for example, as well as after-tax contributions you've made to an employer's savings or thrift plan. Expect to pay income tax on it in the year you receive it. But turn that to your advantage. Tap these savings to fund your income in the first months of your retirement while you give your other assets a chance to generate income to fund future retirement paychecks. Remember, always tax your taxable savings first. Here's your chance.

Create a separate strategy for your stake in your employer's stock. If you're lucky enough to count yourself among the thousands of bull-market millionaires because the company stock in your retirement plan has multiplied in value, you are eligible for special tax treatment that could leave you with a lower tax bill—but only if you take it in a lump-sum distribution (see Chapter 5).

You'll need professional help to figure out what to do with your company stock and when to do it. And you need to get help *before* you take any money at all from your accounts or you'll risk losing your eligibility. You can't withdraw a few thousand shares just to throw yourself a big retirement party in December and still take a lump-sum distribution when you retire in January. You may not be able to take a lump-sum distribution if you've got a loan outstanding from your 401(k) when you retire. It will count as a distribution. The IRS is very clear that this is an all-or-nothing proposition.

David Foster, a Cincinnati-based fee-only financial adviser, works with clients who face this happy problem, because his practice sits squarely in the middle of America's manufacturing heartland. He advises them to take a lump-sum distribution to get the favorable tax treatment, then to decide how much stock they are comfortable owning for the long term, and finally to calculate how much income they need to generate from it. Once the tax is paid on the cost basis of the stock coming out of the plan, some of the stock can be sold and capital gains tax paid on the appreciation (it's only 20 percent versus a maximum 39.6 percent federal income tax rate). Finally, some stock can be held for long-term growth and capital gains tax paid on the appreciation as it is sold.

Designate beneficiaries for each and every account. Read your IRA agreements carefully. Some IRA custodians limit your options for calculating required minimum distributions. That may influence your thinking about your designated beneficiary—or it may lead you to choose another IRA custodian.

Once you begin taking distributions from your retirement accounts, you can change your beneficiary, but you can't take this action to improve—i.e., reduce—your required minimum distributions.

Here's how your assets may look after consolidation:

◆ Rollover IRA to consolidate your workplace savings plan assets (unless you own a big position in your former employer's stock).

◆ Nondeductible IRA.

◆ Deductible IRA.

◆ Roth IRA.

◆ Brokerage account to hold your lump-sum distribution if you have a significant investment in your former employer's stock.

If you roll your retirement assets over into an IRA, you may want to hold them in a brokerage account, even if your money is 100 percent invested in mutual funds. You'll have the flexibility to diversify into individual securities—stocks and bonds—as you manage your assets over time.

STEP TWO: REVIEW YOUR PORTFOLIO ALLOCATION

BEFORE YOU LAUNCH an income plan, review your portfolio allocation. It should reflect both your risk tolerance and your future income needs. In general, it should be more conservative than it was before you retired, but it should not be so conservative that you will miss out on the opportunity for future growth. In fact, some financial experts recommend that you continue to keep as much as 70 percent of your assets in the stock market in retirement. I think that advice is shortsighted. No matter what the statistical averages reveal, this portfolio has to pay for your retirement in real time—not in some theoretical or hypothetical market. Consider this: Insurance companies that sell annuities take your investment dollars and invest in high-grade bonds and blue-chip stocks. That's because they need to cover their risks. You should do the same.

You should have exposure to the stock market, but think about how you will generate adequate retirement income if your stock market investments lose 50 percent of their value during the first year of your retirement. Ridiculous? That's what happened in the early 1970s. In the five years from 1973 to 1977, common stocks lost 0.21 percent. In the decade from 1970 to 1980, they returned just over 3 percent while inflation topped 6.5 percent. It doesn't have to happen again, but I'd rather have a portfolio that can withstand a worst-case event than one that will pump out every possible ounce of return. You may not live commensurably better if your $50,000 annual income has doubled to $100,000 by the time you're 80. But you can bet that if your $50,000 income falls to $25,000 because of an imprudent investment strategy, you will feel the pain.

STEP THREE: CREATE A SEPARATE
RETIREMENT SPENDING ACCOUNT

THIS IS THE ACCOUNT from which you will pay yourself monthly income. Don't mix your investment accounts and your spending account. Don't simply sweep through and collect your dividends and interest income and deposit them into your spending account. Don't treat yourself to a spending spree in a year that you've generated terrific gains. Approach this process methodically, as if you were an employer cutting a paycheck. Offer yourself an income. Promise a raise that will keep up with inflation. Then pour, don't dip.

Here's what I mean: Say you enter retirement with $500,000 that you've rolled over from your employer's 401(k) and profit-sharing plans. You've divided it among stock and bond mutual funds and individual bonds, laddered so that some come due every year—an easy way to manage your interest rate risk. You've also decided to withdraw $30,000 a year or $2,500 a month to supplement your Social Security.

If your portfolio generates more than the $30,000 a year you have targeted for withdrawal, consider yourself ahead of the game, but stick with your plan. Deposit $3,000 into your spending account each month. (You can elect automatic deposit with your investment firm, or a wire transfer if your spending account is at your local bank.)

At least once a year, review your asset allocation and rebalance back to your original stock/bond/cash/international investment mix. If you've further divided your assets along growth/value lines or apportioned your bonds among short-, medium-, and long-term, bring it all back into balance once a year.

In good years, you'll have additional capital to reinvest. In lean years, you'll have to dip into your principal to meet your income needs. If you're consistent with your investment strategy and your withdrawal strategy, your assets should last a lifetime.

HOW MUCH CAN YOU WITHDRAW?

THIS SECTION IS FOR THE delegators and the managers. If you roll your retirement assets into an annuity, the insurance company you purchase it from is charged with figuring out a withdrawal rate that's actuarially sound for the firm and that will meet your required minimum distributions once you're 70½.

However, if you delegate the income-payout process to

a professional, if you set up a systematic withdrawal plan with an investment company, or if you manage your portfolio and create your own retirement paycheck, the rate at which you decide to take money from your savings in the form of retirement income is one of two factors that will determine how long your savings will last.

The problem, of course, is that there's no easy answer. But there are guidelines, such as those provided by the "magic triangle," a device that I stumbled onto early in my financial writing career. Here's how it works: Choose a withdrawal rate from the left side of the triangle; choose an expected investment return from the right side of the triangle. Where the two intersect you'll find the number of years you can expect your assets to last. Inflation has been factored into the triangle, so it assumes that you'll raise your withdrawals each year to make up for rising prices.

As you can see, if your withdrawal rate is modest enough and your investment return is healthy, you may never outlive your savings. Most financial advisers will tell you that 10 percent is too high: Even if you've been accustomed to earning 10 percent a year on your investments, it's unrealistic to think that there won't be some leaner years ahead. And although 3 percent is music to the minds of the most conservative advisers, it's unlikely to keep you on the right side of the law once you are 70½ and have to begin required minimum withdrawals—more on that in the following chapter.

Not surprisingly, then, the consensus seems to fall somewhere between 5 percent and 8 percent. Whether you belong at the top or the bottom of that range is a function of three things:

◆ Your expected investment return.
◆ Whether or not you want to leave money to your heirs.
◆ Whose statistics you believe the most.

For example, withdrawing 8 percent the first year you retire—and increasing your withdrawals over time to account for inflation—requires a healthy investment return. It also means that you're likely to spend down all or

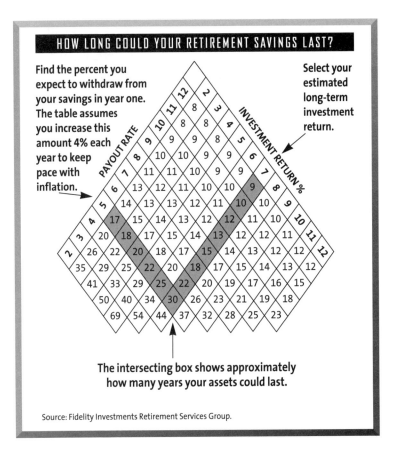

most of your principal in your lifetime. But that's not such a bad idea, says Denver-based financial adviser Judith Shine, if it makes your retirement more comfortable.

By contrast, Boston investment adviser Jim Lowell advises his clients to keep withdrawal rates between 4 and 5 percent. He takes a conservative approach to retirement portfolios, favoring a heavy weighting of high-quality bonds, laddered so that 12 percent mature each year, and solid, domestic blue-chip stocks.

Scott Kuldell, a quantitative analyst at Fidelity Investments, has modeled retirement withdrawal rates and asset allocation strategies and concluded that the best way to increase the probability that you won't outlive your retirement savings is to keep a heavy weighting of stocks in your portfolio—between 50 percent and 70 percent of your assets—*and* keep your withdrawal rates between 4 percent and 5 percent. Kuldell's study was based on monthly investment returns going back to the 1920s and a projected retirement of twenty-five years.

However, what studies like Kuldell's fail to address is the real impact of market volatility. If you have 70 percent of your assets invested in the stock market and it takes a big dive in the early years of your retirement, even a 4 percent withdrawal strategy can wipe out your account in your lifetime. In an ideal world, your investment recovers as the market rebounds. However, because you're taking money out of your account at a regular pace, that leaves fewer and fewer dollars. Money that's gone never has a chance to rebound.

I CAN DO THIS! I'M GETTING TIRED OF DOING THIS! I CAN'T DO THIS ANYMORE!

WHEN IT COMES TO money, investing, and retirement, some things are black and white: For example, I believe it takes more than a skilled investor to manage his or her retirement income: It also takes a strong stomach. I also believe that too many people opt for a fixed annuity too soon because it sounds so simple.

If retirement is an experience that comes in stages, your retirement income strategy should probably change in stages, too. Here's an example. The situation is typical; the story is real; the names are not.

Jim and Beverly Hofstatder met in their 60s. He was a widower and a retired engineer, collecting a modest pension from a major aerospace company from which he had been downsized at age 62. She was divorced and living off the annuity income from a settlement she had received. She also had a modest stock portfolio, which provided her annual travel money. And she owned her own condominium.

When the Hofstatders married at ages 65 and 67, Jim was confident that they could live comfortably on his retirement savings, his Social Security (which he began to collect at 67), and Bev's annuity and stocks. He would continue to manage their assets.

But the year Jim turned 72, the financial markets went a little crazy. His stock funds lost more than 20 percent of their value. For the first time ever, he found himself questioning his investment strategy. Both he and Bev decided they could do with a few less extras until their financial situation stabilized, and they cut back on their withdrawals.

The year Jim turned 77, he noticed that the pay cut he had enforced five years earlier had actually left them with a budget surplus. When he reviewed the figures, he realized that they had traveled less, eaten out less, and spent far less on clothing and household items the year before.

What's more, their investments had done quite well through the market volatility they experienced some years earlier, thanks to Jim's steady hand. But he was getting weary of spending his Saturdays with their monthly investment statement. It was Bev who suggested turning their assets over to a professional manager to free Jim from the burden. They were in the process of interviewing firms that had received good reviews by a local finance columnist when Jim passed away, leaving Bev as the sole heir to their assets. She owed no federal estate tax—you can leave as much as you want to your spouse without worrying about estate tax. But faced with the prospect of filling Jim's shoes, she realized she didn't want the job.

At 76 and on her own, Bev hired the investment manager she and Jim had discussed before his death. He explained his income strategy, which was expected to generate more than enough to cover her estimated monthly expenses when combined with her Social Security survivor benefits. In fact, her adviser estimated that even if she lived another 10 to 15 years, she would have an estate to pass on to her two children and four grandchildren. Bev was confident in the plan, but she was also happy that she had the income from the annuity she received as part of her divorce settlement. It bought her some peace of mind: Regardless of the performance of the financial markets or the skill of her investment manager, she had guaranteed income that would last her lifetime.

And that, as it turned out, was her good fortune. Bev lived to 96. Her investments didn't perform as well as her investment manager had hoped, and there was practically no estate left behind—only the condominium she and Jim had shared. But she continued to collect income from her annuity until the day she died.

CHAPTER

10

Minimum Distributions, MAXIMUM Challenge: When the IRS Says "Show Me the Money"

F YOUR IDEA OF SPENDING your retirement savings is a sense of relief that you're finally at an age when you can take as much as you want without penalty, you probably wonder why there's such a fuss about required minimum distributions. In fact, if your plan is to take as much as possible from your tax-advantaged retirement savings (and do it as fast as you can), you can probably find most of the information you need about required minimum distributions in the overview on page 84 in Chapter 4.

However, if you want to make your retirement savings last as long as possible, you need a strategy to work within the required minimum distribution rules. And if you want to push your withdrawal strategy one step further, to take the absolute minimum you can from your retirement savings during your lifetime so that you can pass as much as possible on to charity or your heirs, you can do it—but only if you understand how to make the rules work for you.

The IRS rules that govern required minimum distributions define when you must begin taking distributions, from what accounts you must take them, and a formula for calculating the amount of your distributions. However, you can either accelerate your required minimum distributions or stretch them out, depending on:

◆ Whether you include a beneficiary in your life expectancy calculation.

◆ How old your beneficiary is.

◆ How you choose to recalculate your life expectancy after your first distribution.

Your choice of beneficiaries and a recalculation method are also important because they can determine how quickly the assets that remain in your retirement account must be withdrawn by your beneficiary or beneficiaries after you're gone.

DON'T MISS THE BEGINNING DATE FOR REQUIRED MINIMUM DISTRIBUTIONS

MARK IT ON YOUR CALENDAR: the day you turn 70½. That's the date when you must begin withdrawals from any IRA that is not a Roth IRA. (Roths are different—you've paid your taxes, now you can take the money whenever you want it.) And, unless you're still working, 70½ is when you've got to begin taking money from your employer's qualified plans. Even if you're still working, if you own more than 5 percent of the company that employs you, you're on for withdrawals beginning at age 70½.

There's one other exception that can help you delay withdrawals from your employer's workplace retirement savings plan, if that's your goal. If you accumulated money in a 403(b) plan prior to 1987, the consensus is that you can delay minimum distributions on these balances until you're 75—although there is no definitive IRS regulation that says so.

You don't actually have to write yourself a check on the day you turn 70½. You can put that off until April 1 of the following year. But you owe yourself a withdrawal for the tax year in which you turned 70½. And you'll be obliged to take two withdrawals in the following year if you put the first one off. Confused? Here's what I mean: You turn 70½ on June 1, 2000. You owe yourself a withdrawal for the year 2000, but you don't actually have to take the money until April 1, 2001. Then you'll have to make your second minimum withdrawal by December 31, 2001.

Does it make a difference whether you take the first two withdrawals in the same year, or take the first one in the year you turn 70½? It could. If it pushes you into a higher tax bracket, you'll have to weigh the additional tax against the benefit of extending tax deferral for another few months.

What happens if you don't take your required minimum distribution when you are supposed to? The penalty is one of the stiffest levied by the IRS: 50 percent. If you skip out on the withdrawal entirely, you'll pay a 50 percent

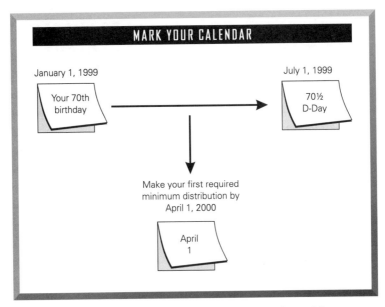

MARK YOUR CALENDAR

January 1, 1999

Your 70th birthday

July 1, 1999

70½ D-Day

Make your first required minimum distribution by April 1, 2000

April 1

penalty on the amount you should have taken. If your error was in not taking enough, you'll pay 50 percent on the difference between what you should have taken and what you did take.

In either case, you'll have to actually take the full distribution and pay tax on it. And you'll have to take any distribution that is due in the year your error is discovered. Even if you took an amount greater than your required minimum withdrawal last year, you can't carry anything over to the following year. The IRS is entirely inflexible about the timing of required minimum withdrawals.

What if you haven't taken your minimum withdrawals because you simply didn't understand the rules? Lou Beckerman with Northeast Planning Services, Inc., a Massachusetts benefits administration firm, says there's no real mechanism to find people who are behind; and unless you are audited, you may escape notice—at least for a time. Clark Blackman II, Deloitte & Touche LLP's national director of investment advisory development, says the IRS can and typically will waive this penalty when the failure is inadvertent and you take steps to distribute the required amount immediately.

MAXIMIZE INCOME OR TRANSFER WEALTH? CHOOSE A STRATEGY TO MATCH YOUR GOALS

IF YOU FEEL THAT YOU'VE saved enough for a comfortable retirement, you may be surprised to learn that the choices you make about required minimum distributions can either help you get as much income as you can for as long as possible (read: delay income tax for as long as possible!)—or get in your way.

The withdrawal rules establish a minimum rate at which you'll have to draw down your savings after you're 70½. But the choices you make about calculating your life expectancy, whom you choose as a beneficiary, and whether or not to include your beneficiary in the calculation can make a significant difference in how *minimum* those required distributions are, how long they will last, and what happens to the assets left in your accounts after you're gone.

Your required minimum distributions are based on two factors: the value of your retirement savings accounts at the end of the year and your life expectancy, which you can find in the tables in Appendix E of IRS Publication 590. Or ask your accountant. For example, if you're 70 and the life expectancy tables project that you're going to live another sixteen years, you simply divide your account value on December 31 by your life expectancy to arrive at the amount of your required minimum distribution.

Next year, you'll repeat the calculation based on the new value of your account. But what about your life expectancy? If you subtract one year for every year you take a required minimum distribution, and you're still around after sixteen years, your retirement savings will be gone. Mercifully, that limitation has not escaped notice by the IRS, which offers an alternative. Instead of being locked into a table that takes away one year every year, you can choose to *recalculate* your life expectancy each year.

YOU CAN SPEED UP OR SLOW DOWN YOUR INCOME

If You Want Your Retirement Savings to Provide . . .

More income at a faster rate:	Less income at a slower rate:
Fix your life expectancy	Recalculate your life expectancy

Here's how much you would be required to withdraw from a $100,000 account earning 8 percent.

Withdrawals begin at age 70½:

YEAR	LIFE EXPECTANCY	WITHDRAWAL	LIFE EXPECTANCY	WITHDRAWAL
1	15	$6,667	15.3	$6,536
2	14	$7,200	14.6	$6,914
3	13	$7,776	13.9	$7,306
4	12	$8,398	13.2	$7,711
5	11	$9,070	12.5	$8,128
6	10	$9,796	11.9	$8,483

Using the alternate recalculation method, your life expectancy in the second year is 15.3 instead of 15 with the fixed method.

You can see what happens over time, depending on the calculation method you choose. With the fixed method, your required minimum distributions are higher and your money runs out faster. With the recalculation method, your withdrawals are lower and last longer. In fact, using the recalculation method, your money won't run out until you're approximately 110.

It's a good idea to plan your strategy to satisfy required minimum distributions at least a year before you're required to begin taking them—the year you turn 70½. That will give you a chance to weigh the alternatives, to make sure your Individual Retirement Account (IRA) or retirement plan custodian will allow you to execute the strategy you choose (and to move your money someplace else if it does not), and to give appropriate written notice about your choices to the IRS, if it's required.

GET MORE MILEAGE WHEN YOU CALCULATE WITH A BENEFICIARY

THERE'S ANOTHER WAY to stretch out your minimum distributions. If you've named a "designated" beneficiary for your retirement account, i.e., one that the IRS recognizes as having a life span of its own—an individual, or a trust in which the individual beneficiaries of the trust are easily identified, not a charity or your estate—you can include your beneficiary's life expectancy in your annual calculation and drive your required minimum withdrawal even lower.

In fact, because the method you choose to calculate your withdrawals only establishes a minimum amount, and you can always take more money out of your retirement account if you want, most financial advisers will tell you it *always* makes sense to calculate your withdrawals in conjunction with a beneficiary—even if you're single.

Most married couples name their spouse as their retirement account beneficiary. Clearly that's what the IRS had in mind by offering couples more withdrawal options if they do. But where there is flexibility, there is also complexity. Here's what I mean: The IRS says you can use a fixed-term calculation for both life expectancies; you can recalculate both life expectancies; or you can recalculate one and used a fixed-term life expectancy for the other. But, in effect, the IRS says you just can't have it both ways: Generally speaking, if you want to slow down withdrawals over your lifetime, they're going to pick up after you're gone. If you're willing to accelerate them a little during your lifetime, your beneficiary has a shot at extending them if he or she outlives you.

For example, if you know you're going to need sizable annual withdrawals to live on, consider using the fixed-term calculation for both life expectancies. It will bind you to slightly higher withdrawals during your lifetime. However, regardless of who dies first, the other spouse can continue to take withdrawals over the combined life expectancy.

WEIGHING THE TRADEOFFS

IF YOU ELECT . . .	THE EFFECT ON YOUR REQUIRED MINIMUM WITHDRAWALS IS . . .
Single life expectancy	Higher required withdrawals
Joint life expectancy	Lower required withdrawals
Fixed-term life expectancy	Higher required withdrawals
Recalculate life expectancy	Lower required withdrawals
Joint life expectancy, fixed term	Higher withdrawals now, lower later for surviving spouse
Joint life expectancy, recalculate	Lower withdrawals now, higher later for surviving spouse
Joint life expectancy, owner uses fixed, spouse recalculates	Lower withdrawals now, but higher if your spouse dies first
Joint life expectancy, owner recalculates, spouse uses fixed	Lower withdrawals now; your spouse can roll over into an IRA if you die first

The best way to minimize your withdrawals during your lifetime is to recalculate both life expectancies. However, if your spouse dies first, you'll then have to accelerate withdrawals because your life expectancy reverts back to a fixed term. If you die first, your spouse makes out better because the IRS offers your surviving spouse the option of rolling the balance of the retirement assets into an IRA, choosing a new distribution method, and naming a new beneficiary. However, if you both die at the same time, all the money has to come out in short order because neither one of you has any life expectancy left.

It's that last "what if" that pushes Bob Keebler, a CPA with Schumaker Romenesko & Associates in Green Bay, Wisconsin, to favor a hybrid calculation. Keebler says your best all-around shot for extending withdrawals over two lifetimes is to recalculate *your* life expectancy, but not your spouse's. That way you'll preserve the IRA rollover option for your spouse if you die first. But if your spouse dies first, you won't be penalized. You'll continue with the same life expectancy factor as before, and your distributions won't accelerate—they stay the same.

What if you don't name a spouse as your beneficiary, because you're not married or because your spouse's retirement income needs have been adequately covered by other accounts? For starters, you won't have the option of recalculating your beneficiary's life expectancy: That option is only available to a spouse. And if you name a significantly younger beneficiary—whether or not it's your spouse—don't get too excited about the prospects for arriving at a long joint life expectancy factor. You can't use more than a ten-year difference. For example, if you're 70 and you designate your 35-year-old daughter as your beneficiary, the IRS says she's 60. (But it doesn't say you have to tell her that.)

So why bother naming a younger beneficiary? Two reasons: First, if you have substantial assets in your retirement account—$1 million or more—you could end up creating a future estate tax problem if your spouse is your beneficiary. That's why many people choose a child or a grandchild, a niece or a nephew. Second, if you choose a younger beneficiary, that individual can revert to his or her actual life expectancy after you die, reduced by the number of years you've been making withdrawals—which means taxes can be postponed and withdrawals spread out for many years to come. If you name more than one younger person as a beneficiary, you'll have to use the life expectancy of the oldest child. In fact, if your goal is to provide for more than one beneficiary of a younger generation, your best strategy may be to divide your assets into multiple accounts and make each child the beneficiary of one account. That way, each can calculate withdrawals over his or her own life expectancy when the time comes.

One more point: Think twice about naming a grandchild as beneficiary if your account is worth more than $1 million. It will probably be hit with a 55 percent generation-skipping estate tax. There are better ways to provide for your heirs and pay less tax.

If all this sounds complicated to you, you're right. The

calculation of joint life expectancies alone—if you choose to recalculate yours, but not those of your joint beneficiaries—is a multistep exercise. I wouldn't touch it. And there's more: If you've got more than one type of retirement account—a 401(k), for example, plus a tax-sheltered annuity and several IRAs—you have to deal with the required minimum withdrawal calculation for each type of account. You can aggregate your IRA balances and figure the minimum distribution for your IRAs and you can aggregate tax-sheltered annuity 403(b)s. But if you have multiple 401(k)s or profit-sharing plans, you have to figure the minimum distribution for and take the minimum distribution from each plan. That said, it's important to understand that there may be estate planning reasons for not aggregating accounts even where the IRS allows it. If you name different beneficiaries for different accounts, it's not only possible but probable that you will have different joint life expectancies for the purpose of recalculating your withdrawals. Does this process ever end?

If you've been on the fence regarding professional advice as part of your planning, the required minimum withdrawal process may push you over the edge. Keebler says that no matter how little or how much money you have in your retirement accounts, you need more than general financial guidance—you need expert tax advice on how to elect a beneficiary and choose among the life expectancy calculation/recalculation options. If your accounts are simple, if you leave everything to your spouse, the most common approach is to choose joint life expectancy with recalculation for yourself and a fixed term for your spouse. However, every family has its own issues, and that may not be the right choice for you. Certainly if you have a desire to designate different beneficiaries for your different plans, or for different accounts within plans, you need the help of a knowledgeable retirement professional. And you need it before you lock yourself into any of these choices.

Because lock yourself in is exactly what you'll do: For example, if you're going to use the fixed-term calculation method, you have to notify the IRS of your intentions in writing before April 1 of the year after you turn 70½—the same date that you're required to make your first withdrawal. And once you start using either the fixed-term or recalculation method, you can't change it.

What's more, you *can* change your beneficiary, but once you begin taking withdrawals after you're 70½, you *can't* change your beneficiary to your advantage. You can't slow down distributions. However, you can speed them inadvertently by naming an *older* beneficiary if your original beneficiary dies. One more consideration: If you choose the fixed-term calculation, you'll forfeit the flexibility to roll over the balance of your retirement account to an annuity, an option that most people should keep open for their later years.

DYING TO GET AT YOUR MONEY

SO FAR, ALL THESE RULES assume that you live to 70½ and begin withdrawals in your lifetime. If you die before you begin to take required minimum withdrawals from your retirement plan, there is at least one additional wrinkle to the rules. If you haven't chosen a designated beneficiary, the IRS offers a five-year period over which withdrawals can be spread, versus one year if you die after you've started withdrawals. A designated beneficiary can also take advantage of the five-year window or elect to spread withdrawals over his or her life expectancy, provided distributions begin by the end of the year following the year in which you die. Again, your spouse gets special treatment: He or she can roll over the money into an IRA.

Your Retirement
ASSETS
as Part of
Your Estate

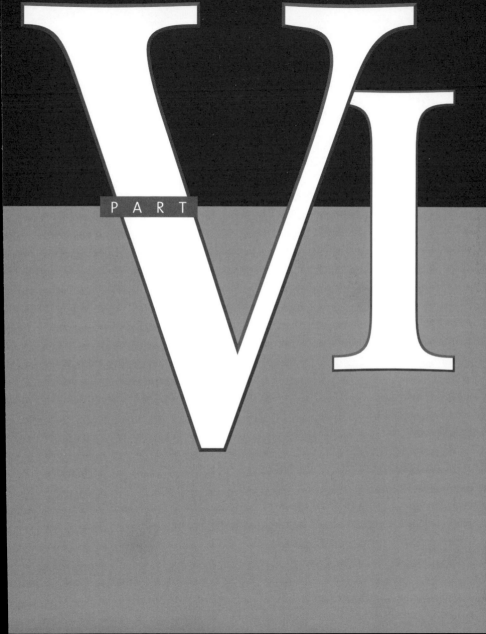

PART

VI

CHAPTER

Who Gets Your Retirement ASSETS after You're Gone?

HEN I started this book, I hoped that what I had to say would help people who had saved $100,000 or more in their retirement plans from making big mistakes that would cost them money or the right to remain flexible over time. I had heard stories of people who had amassed a million dollars or more in their accounts, but I thought they were exceptions. Now I'm not so sure. It's no longer difficult to imagine that tax-advantaged retirement accounts will be the single largest asset most of us will accumulate during our working years—worth more than our homes and even more than our pension plans, for those who are still lucky enough to have them. Substantial assets create the opportunity for a lifetime of retirement income: Isn't that what we're all hoping for? But without proper planning, they also have the potential to create substantial headaches for our heirs.

If you have at least $500,000 in retirement plan assets, this chapter and the following one can be especially useful. You want to make choices that will preserve as much as you can for the people you care about, help them to keep their future tax bills low—and delay those bills as long as possible. And if you have charitable goals in mind, you want to make sure that your estate plan is structured to meet them.

That said, I want to make clear that this is not a book on estate planning. I would be stretching my own credentials to suggest that you can read these chapters and walk away with all the answers to your estate planning issues. That's a job for an estate planning professional. However, if I can raise the important issues so that you can ask intelligent questions, I think you can avoid some obvious mistakes and be one step closer to keeping your retirement assets working for generations to come.

CHOOSE YOUR RETIREMENT PLAN BENEFICIARIES WITH FUTURE TAXES IN MIND

WHEN YOUR RETIREMENT assets are part of an estate that tops $650,000—the amount of your lifetime exemption from federal estate and gift tax and a moving target that rises to $1 million in 2006—you have two worries. The first is how to help your heirs manage the future income tax liability on your account. Everyone has to worry about that. And by choosing your beneficiary and life expectancy calculation method wisely, you can usually achieve your goal, whether it is to maximize income in your lifetime or spread it out as long as possible for your heirs. The second worry, however, is your estate tax liability—because retirement account assets are particularly vulnerable.

Here's what I mean: If you're married, you can give your retirement assets a first line of defense by passing them on to your spouse, who, if he or she is a U.S. citizen, can take advantage of the unlimited marital deduction and inherit your assets free of estate tax. As your spouse withdraws money from your retirement assets, there'll be income tax to deal with, but nothing more.

But if the account value exceeds $650,000 when your surviving spouse passes away, or if you pass your retirement plan assets on to someone other than your spouse, both estate and income tax will be due on the assets they inherit.

This gets complicated, so take a look at what happens to a $1 million retirement account in this example offered by Eva Ribarits, vice president of estate planning at Fidelity Investments: First it is subject to federal estate tax of up to 55 percent or $550,000. (That's the *highest* estate tax rate. Federal estate tax begins at 37 percent.) Then there's the federal income tax liability to the beneficiaries on the $1 million retirement asset, assuming they choose to take it all at once, which amounts to another $396,000.

Add it up, and nearly 100 percent of your retirement plan assets could be paid out in taxes. Even the IRS admits that's not fair, says Ribarits. To soften the blow, it allows your heirs to reduce their income tax liability with an income tax deduction equal to the estate tax liability paid on the income within the retirement asset—in this case, $550,000. As a result, your beneficiaries would be subject to income tax on only $450,000 of the retirement plan asset. If it were taxed at the current maximum federal income tax rate of 39.6 percent, the total taxes on the $1 million would be brought down to $728,200.

That's a good deal, you ask? Well, it's better than a tax bill of $946,000. But it does suggest that you or your heirs should consider alternatives that could reduce—or at least spread out—the tax liability so that more benefit can be gained from these assets.

One option, of course, is for your heirs to take advantage of their ability to stretch out withdrawals over their life expectancy if you've done the right thing and elected a joint life expectancy calculation. For example, if your ten-year-old child inherits your million-dollar IRA and distributions are spread out over her life expectancy, the child will pay taxes at her current tax rate. By the time she's in college, the income from the Individual Retirement Account (IRA) will easily foot the bill for a top-notch private education, even at today's rising costs. And given a life expectancy of over sixty years, an account that continues to compound tax-deferred each year could generate millions of additional dollars in income over her lifetime.

CONSIDER A TRUST AS THE BENEFICIARY OF YOUR RETIREMENT PLAN ASSETS

THANKS TO A 1997 CHANGE in the income tax regulations, you can name a revocable trust as the beneficiary of your retirement plan assets and get the same advantages that used to be available only to individuals who established an irrevocable trust. Why is a revocable trust a better deal? You can alter the terms of the trust, change the beneficiaries, and even eliminate it altogether while you're alive. That makes it easier for you to retain control over your assets in your lifetime and to make changes when the people whom you care about disappoint you along the way. However, in order for a revocable trust to qualify for special treatment under the new IRS guidelines, it has to meet four important criteria:

◆ The trust must be valid under state law.

◆ The beneficiaries of the retirement plan asset must be clearly identifiable from the trust document.

◆ A copy of the trust document or a list of trust beneficiaries must be provided to the retirement plan administrator.

◆ The trust, by its terms, must become irrevocable on the death of the retirement plan owner.

The new rule enlarges the estate planning options available to individuals with substantial retirement plan assets because:

◆ It gives them a measure of control they didn't have before.

◆ It allows them to apply estate tax savings strategies such as the **CREDIT SHELTER TRUST** and the **MARITAL TRUST** to retirement plan assets. For example, if the assets you have outside of your retirement plan fall short of $650,000—that's the magic number that you can pass on to any individual, estate and gift tax free, also known as the unified credit equivalent—you can transfer a portion of your retirement plan assets (whatever it would take to get up to $650,000) into a credit shelter or bypass trust without accelerating the income tax liability on your retirement assets. You can name your spouse as the sole beneficiary. Your spouse can take income immediately or postpone it until the date you would have been required to begin minimum withdrawals—the April 1 after you would have turned 70½.

When your surviving spouse dies, any future income can be spread over the life expectancy of the oldest beneficiary—typically, your children—and whatever is left after the second-line beneficiaries have died can transfer to your grandchildren, who will have up to five years to withdraw the remaining assets. Eva Ribarits, vice president of estate planning at Fidelity, advises clients to use the credit shelter trust for retirement plan assets only if no other assets are available for funding this trust. That's because a credit shelter or bypass trust limits your spouse's distribution options: He or she can't elect a rollover. Perhaps even more important, the assets are subject to income tax when received by the trust, thereby reducing the amount passing estate tax free to the participant's children or other beneficiaries when the spouse dies. Had the assets been paid to the spouse or a trust designed to qualify for the marital deduction, the income tax paid on the benefits would have reduced the amount subject to estate tax when the spouse dies. However the benefit of deferral may outweigh the income tax cost.

You can also transfer your retirement plan assets into a marital trust. This is a useful option for folks who are on a second or third marriage and want to provide income for the current spouse, but also ensure that the assets are eventually passed on to the children of an earlier marriage. The catch is that the income from a marital trust must be paid out annually, so your spouse won't have the option of postponing taxable income into the future.

Like so many options, there are tradeoffs to keep in mind when choosing a trust. With a credit shelter trust, you get more control over the timing of income. With a marital trust, you get more control over the assets. But you can't have it both ways.

IF YOU ARE CHARITABLY INCLINED

OUR FEDERAL TAX LAWS encourage charitable giving.
And although that alone won't transform a Scrooge into a
Carnegie, they will make you think twice. If you name a
charity as the beneficiary of your retirement plan assets,
you'll bypass several levels of taxation:

◆ Neither you nor any beneficiary will pay federal income
  tax, which could amount to 39.6 percent on any distributions that come from your plan.

◆ Your estate will avoid up to 55 percent in estate tax.

◆ No other taxes will be due: no generation-skipping
  taxes, no income tax to the estate or named beneficiaries.

There is one disadvantage: If you name a charity as your
beneficiary, it won't satisfy the IRS's designated beneficiary
rule. That means you can only use a single life expectancy
factor to calculate your required minimum distributions,
which will speed up your withdrawals. You could give your
retirement plan assets directly to a charity during your lifetime, but this doesn't work as well for you. The IRS will
assume that you first took a distribution (subject to income
tax) and then made the contribution. That would give you
the right to claim a charitable deduction against your
income, subject to certain limitations. (Generally speaking, you can deduct a contribution of up to 50 percent of
your adjusted gross income and carry the balance forward
for five years.) But you could still end up with a significant
tax bill.

A better approach is to bequeath your retirement plan
assets to a charity at your death. The charity doesn't pay
income tax. There's no income tax due from you. And
the full value of your bequest will be deductible against the
value of the estate for estate tax purposes.

Sometimes it's psychologically hard to bypass your family
and give your assets to charity, even though you know that
most of your wealth would end up with the IRS if you left
it to your family members. However, if your retirement
plan assets total a million dollars or more, there is a way to

accomplish both goals, says Eva Ribarits: You leave your retirement plan assets to your spouse. Your spouse, in turn, specifies that on his or her death the assets will fund a private family foundation. Your children, grandchildren, and great-grandchildren sit on the board of directors and receive an annual income for the role they play in running the foundation. Ribarits calls this the "charitable family business."

There are laws that govern how much the foundation must disperse each year—at least 5 percent of its income. The salaries paid to directors have to be *reasonable,* which is defined less in terms of absolute dollars than as a function of the directors activities in the service of the foundation.

It's important to stay well within the rules: You can't eat away at the foundation's assets and turn it into a vehicle for distributing wealth to the directors. Try it and you could get hit with excise taxes. The IRS could disallow the foundation's tax-exempt status.

But if you play by the rules, there's plenty of opportunity to satisfy your charitable goals and ensure that your family reaps the benefits of some of the assets you have worked so hard to accumulate. Ribarits had a client who used a $10 million nest egg to fund a private foundation and even put restrictions on *when* foundation directors/heirs could receive income. The family wrote into the foundation document that the value of foundation assets had to reach a certain size before board members would be compensated. What's reasonable income for a director? It could be $15,000 a year—or $150,000. It depends on how well the foundation's assets perform. There's no honor in holding back money that is above and beyond the foundation's mission to distribute a mere 5 percent of the income of the assets. According to Ribarits, the challenge to the foundation directors is to make sure it's always earning enough money to keep its seed money intact, disburse 5 percent as a gift to nonprofit organizations, and then divvy up the income reasonably among the directors.

IS A ROTH RIGHT OR WRONG
FOR YOUR ESTATE?

IN CHAPTER 5, WE TALKED about the mechanics and timing of converting to a Roth IRA, the retirement savings
vehicle that turns the tables on the traditional tax benefits
of retirement savings plans. There's no income tax deduction up front. But after you turn 59½ once you've had a
Roth IRA established for five years, you can take income
tax-free withdrawals forever. If you have a traditional IRA,
you can convert to a Roth IRA by paying the income tax
due on the assets you convert.

Bob Keebler, a CPA with Schumaker Romenesko &
Associates in Green Bay, Wisconsin, and the author of the
American Institute of Certified Public Accountants publication *Making the Most of the Roth IRA*, tells his clients there
are at least a half-dozen reasons to convert to a Roth IRA.
(Now that the opportunity to spread your tax bill on a
Roth over four years is past, there is one less.) But Keebler
says that the most important ones are those that relate to
the flexibility you can get from a Roth:

◆ No required minimum withdrawals.
◆ The freedom to change your beneficiary after you're 70½.

By converting to a Roth IRA, you can bypass all the complicated life expectancy calculations that are associated
with required minimum withdrawals. And because they
drive the rate at which you have to take money out if your
beneficiary dies before you do, or at which your heirs have
to take money out, you're somewhat at the mercy of fate:
You can do your best to structure a withdrawal plan from
a traditional IRA and still be undone by the untimely
death of a beneficiary.

Keebler also points out that by paying the taxes on assets
converted to a Roth IRA during your lifetime, you remove
assets that would be subject to estate tax and perhaps also
lower the applicable estate tax rate, since it ranges from
37 percent to 55 percent.

It's the nonfinancial benefits that make a Roth so attractive, says Keebler, although there may also be a slight financial advantage to converting in your lifetime. "You've got to pay income taxes on your IRA assets sometime. It doesn't matter when you pay them."

Eva Ribarits, Fidelity's vice president of estate planning, has a different point of view. Says Ribarits, you can't ignore the timing of taxes. If you convert traditional IRA assets to a Roth IRA when you are 60, using outside funds that were earning an annual rate of 8 percent, it could take approximately twenty-two years for you to break even. "A 60-year-old doesn't have a twenty-two-year life expectancy!"

Ribarits is skeptical about the Roth conversion hype in general. She points out that for decades financial firms have been urging clients to save in a tax-deferred manner. Now, all of a sudden, investors are being encouraged to accelerate their tax payments. "I have yet to see an example where conversion makes sense for an older taxpayer," she declares.

But what about the notion that you'll reduce your estate tax by taking money now to pay income tax on your converted assets? Keebler and Ribarits also see this issue differently. Keebler says it's pure math. A million-dollar IRA balance gets hit with $550,000 in estate tax and, after income tax and allowing for the deduction for the estate tax paid, is worth about $229,700 to the beneficiary. Take a Roth worth $604,000 ($1 million minus $396,000 paid in income tax) less estate tax of $332,000—but no offset, because income tax has been paid—and the beneficiary comes out about $42,000 ahead with $271,800.

But Ribarits says you've got to look at the estate tax and income tax issues separately: Estate tax is an issue for the lawyer and the estate planner to settle in advance. And what about the opportunity cost of the $400,000 that was used to pay income tax on the conversion? If it had earned 8 percent for just two years before the death of the account holder, the beneficiary would come out ahead.

CHAPTER

12

When You
Inherit
RETIREMENT
PLAN ASSETS

ETWEEN WILLS, TAXES, AND time limits on key decisions, it's hard to imagine how people find the time to grieve properly at the death of a loved one in a world obsessed by rules, laws, and forms. Yet, if you are the beneficiary of someone's retirement plan assets, it's important to understand your options before you have to make decisions that could be costly and irrevocable. Whether you are the beneficiary of the retirement plan assets of your spouse, a parent, or someone unrelated by birth, you may have to make your decisions with the IRS clock ticking.

Here are some general rules to keep in mind: If you're a spouse, you have more options than if you're not. If you are a child or grandchild, you will want to think about whether you want quick access to the money that's been left you or whether you can afford to let it grow tax-deferred. If the account owner had already begun taking minimum distributions from the plan or receiving annuity payments, your options are different. If there's more than $650,000 involved and you're not the account owner's spouse, the estate will have to settle up its tax issues before you ever see any money. If more than $50,000 is involved, consider seeking professional advice before you make any decisions at all. And don't count on anything happening quickly.

WHEN YOU INHERIT AN IRA

WHEN MY FRIEND Karen Ernst lost her mother in the summer of 1997, she learned that she was the sole beneficiary of her mother's Individual Retirement Account (IRA). Although Karen had worked in the financial services industry for nearly fifteen years, it occurred to her that she didn't know what her options were regarding her mother's account. After several visits to the financial services firm that held her mother's IRA, she was told she might as well just take the money. After all, it wasn't a king's ransom. However, taxes are taxes, and the advice Karen received oversimplified the matter. She could have spread her withdrawals—and her tax liability—over her entire life expectancy. Or, at minimum, she could have taken the money out over five years. In either case the funds would have had more time to grow free of taxes.

The IRS offers little guidance on what to do with an inherited IRA. And many IRA providers are inadequately prepared to handle questions or transactions involving inherited IRAs. That's partly because IRAs were designed for retirement savings not for wealth transfer and partly because the issues are relatively new, says Kenneth P. Brier, a Boston attorney who specializes in retirement account issues. If you are the surviving spouse of the IRA owner, you have more options and more flexibility (see page 258). However, if you are a child or a grandchild or you are unrelated to the IRA owner, your best bet is to stretch out withdrawals over your life expectancy. If it's a small amount and it seems like a hassle to stay on top of it for twenty or thirty years, don't be so sure it's not worth it. If you inherit a $20,000 IRA at age 40, tax-deferred compounding at 8 percent can turn it into $115,000 worth of income over your lifetime, after which you would still have $57,000 remaining in your account. At minimum, consider electing the rule that allows you to spread withdrawals over five years.

You may want to change the investment mix, especially if you're a lot younger than the original account holder. You may want a more aggressive strategy. You should also be able to transfer the account from one IRA provider to another—but don't count on getting a lot of help.

If you choose to take the money out over your life expectancy, be sure to take the first withdrawal by December 31 of the year following the death of the IRA owner, or you'll be stuck with an accelerated withdrawal schedule.

One more warning: Don't change the name on the account. That converts the inheritance into a withdrawal in the eyes of the IRS, and the whole amount is taxable in the year you take it.

If you inherit an IRA, it's important for you to establish your own beneficiary for the assets in the account. But you're not the account owner, so technically you can't designate a beneficiary for the account. Brier, however, feels that is open to interpretation. However, to ensure that money ends up where it is wanted, he advises clients to name their beneficiaries in their wills. Brier's firm typically drafts its own beneficiary forms, customized to each individual's situation, but he admits that he's often had to push his way up the organization chain of command to ensure that an IRA provider will honor them.

The rules for inheriting other types of qualified retirement plans are similar to those for IRAs. But keep in mind that the tax issues associated with highly appreciated employer securities are complex. You should seek professional advice before you make any decisions about inherited appreciated securities.

SPOUSES ARE DIFFERENT

FEW FINANCIAL TRANSACTIONS are worry-free, but generally speaking, it's easier to settle the benefits you're entitled to from your spouse's employer's defined benefit plan than it is to settle those of any other retirement plan asset you inherit. Companies have decades of experience in administering these plans. Plan documents must provide details about the options available to surviving spouses, and most elections are made when the plan participant commences employment.

If your spouse was vested, you should be entitled to collect a lifetime annuity, or you may be offered a lump-sum distribution based on the estimated value of your spouse's retirement benefits when he or she passed away, even if your spouse was years away from normal retirement age. If your spouse was already collecting pension income, you'll be entitled to continue to receive income, although perhaps at a reduced rate, unless you forfeited that right in writing.

INHERITING YOUR SPOUSE'S IRA

HOWEVER, AS MORE AMERICANS are accumulating retirement savings in their IRAs, or rolling over retirement assets from employer-sponsored plans to IRAs, there's a new generation of questions, problems, and answers that few people think about until they are actually faced with the situation.

If you are the beneficiary of your spouse's IRA and your spouse dies before starting required minimum withdrawals at 70½, you'll have about a year to decide what to do with the money. You can:

◆ Take all the money out of the account.

◆ Withdraw the money based on your life expectancy. The IRS includes life expectancy tables in Publication 590. Your accountant can help.

◆ Delay withdrawals until the year your spouse would have turned 70½ and then take the money out based on your own life expectancy.

◆ Roll the assets over into your own IRA, in which case you become the owner, name your own beneficiary, and delay minimum withdrawals until you're 70½. You have to be the sole beneficiary of the account to have this option available.

Unless you really need the money, the last option usually makes the most sense. First of all, the whole idea behind retirement savings is that they were designed to provide retirement income, so why take the money out and pay tax on it any faster than you have to? Second, future financial transactions are a lot easier if the account is in your name. You can move it to another financial institution with fewer questions and hassles.

Of course, if you are younger than 59½ and need the money, you are entitled to make penalty-free withdrawals from your deceased spouse's retirement plan or IRA only if you leave it as it is. Then you can roll it over into your own IRA once you turn 59½—or at least there's nothing official that says you can't treat your inherited IRA this way. However, there have been several private letter rulings that raise questions about this strategy. It makes sense to get an opinion before you do anything.

Here's another point to consider if you survive a significantly younger spouse: It could be worth it to delay distributions until the year in which your spouse would have turned 70½. In fact, depending on the age gap—say you're 65 and your spouse was 45—you may never have to take required minimum withdrawals in your lifetime. If you don't need your retirement savings to live on, you could create a significant nest egg for your heirs with this strategy.

If your spouse had already started making required withdrawals, there's another reason to roll over to your own account. Your spouse had to choose whether to take the assets using a single or joint life expectancy and also select a method for recalculating his or her life expectancy. If you keep the IRA in your deceased spouse's name, you'll have to continue to take distributions under the method your spouse chose.

No matter what your withdrawal strategy, if you choose to leave the assets in your spouse's IRA, be sure to designate a beneficiary for these assets in your will. However, because you're not the account holder, there's no life-expectancy payout available to the second-line beneficiary—only the options to take the money as a lump sum or over five years. That's why it's usually a good idea to roll the assets over into your own IRA.

And remember, if you choose to withdraw money using your own life expectancy, the clock is ticking. You've got a year plus to make your first withdrawal: by December 31 of the year after your spouse's death.

RESOURCES

GETTING ADVICE

OVER THE COURSE OF WRITING this book, I have spoken with dozens of investment advisers, tax specialists, estate planners, and personal finance experts who understand both the big picture and the minutiae of turning retirement plan savings into lifetime income and wealth for your heirs. But when I think of 77 million baby boomers retiring in the next two decades, I shudder to think where they will all find the advice they need to make the most out of their retirement plans. Bob Keebler, a CPA with Schumaker Romenesko & Associates in Green Bay, Wisconsin, may have been kidding when he said there are about fifteen people in the whole country who are both smart enough to understand this stuff and articulate enough to make it understandable to the rest of us. He didn't say he was one of them, but I will. So are the others whose names appear in this book.

Do you need professional advice? Jonathan Pond, author of dozens of books on personal finance and a regular on PBS's *Nightly Business Report,* says you need it if you have a lot of money and you especially need it if you don't. I think that's true. Even if you have $20,000 in an IRA, if you're uncertain about what you can do with it, when you should, and what the tax consequences are, it's worth one session with a financial planner. It may cost you $250. Or it may be help you can get from your employer. Polaroid, for example, offers departing employees access to a financial planning package created by the accounting firm Ernst & Young. There's a modest fee involved, but corporate benefits manager Bill Hubert thinks it's worth it.

Choosing an adviser is anything but a scientific process, although I believe the best resources have a way of making themselves known. I wouldn't put all my faith in one of the annual lists run by magazines such as *SmartMoney* or *Worth* magazine. But if you find a name that shows up there and also in the local press, you've made a start. Yet sometimes an expert is more expert at cultivating press contacts than in running his or her business, so be careful. On the other hand, someone who is articulate enough to be quoted frequently is probably also good at explaining concepts and options to clients.

If there's something unusual about your retirement savings, don't stop your search until you find someone who is expert in your problem. For example, Procter & Gamble employees who have found their way to Michael Chasnoff and David Foster, both of whom specialize in accounts that are heavy with appreciated employer securities, have been fortunate. Likewise for educators who have sought the counsel of Janet Briaud, a Texas-based financial planner who specializes in retirement planning for career educators. If your affairs are complicated, this is not a job for a generalist—not even a smart, hard-working one. You wouldn't put your cancer in the hands of your general practitioner. Give your retirement plan assets the same consideration.

And most certainly, if you have at least $650,000 in assets between your home, your personal savings, and your retirement savings plans, you need to have an estate plan that will help you make your savings last for your children and grandchildren.

The books, newsletters, and Web sites that follow can also help you find answers, expand your knowledge, and avoid costly mistakes so that the nest egg you have worked so hard to build will always be there when you need it. I've taken some care to select the best examples I know in each category. There is no lack of information today. The trick is to find resources that are knowledgeable and easy to understand.

BOOKS

YOU DON'T NEED A DEGREE in personal finance. You don't need an entire investment library. You *do* need to understand the basics. And if you're going to manage your own retirement assets—even as a manager/delegator—you need to understand how the financial markets work. With that in mind, here are some resources that could make your life easier:

A Commonsense Guide to Your 401(k) by Mary Rowland (Bloomberg, 1997). Rowland has written about 401(k)s with the reader in mind. More than a list of rules and regulations, the book tackles problems, strategies, and real-life situations. All of a sudden, there seem to be dozens of books on 401(k)s. This is the best.

Creating Retirement Income by Virginia B. Morris (McGraw-Hill, 1999). A sound-bite approach to retirement income planning. Understand the bias before you get started: The book was written in conjunction with the National Association of Variable Annuities. However, Morris knows how to take complicated concepts and break them into meaningful nuggets without losing their bite. Lots of graphics; a practical, slim format; easy reading.

The Inheritor's Handbook: A Definitive Guide for Beneficiaries by Dan Rottenberg (Bloomberg, 1999). An estimated 60 million Americans are due to receive an inheritance in the next decade. If you're one of them, here's a book that can help you plan for your new wealth, then put it to work for the next generation.

Investing During Retirement: The Vanguard Guide to Managing Your Retirement Assets (Irwin, 1996). The scope of this book is broader than that of the rest, but that's its strength. It picks up with a question—"Can you afford to retire?"—then walks you through some basic investment and mutual fund principles, and provides a nice overview of withdrawal options and estate planning.

The New Commonsense Guide to Mutual Funds by Mary Rowland (Bloomberg, 1998). Organization is everything. Rowland takes the complexities of mutual fund investing and turns them into 75 "dos and don'ts" that make it easy to find just the information you need. This new edition is a paperback.

If there's a gap in your financial education and you don't know where to start, here are some good choices:

Learn to Earn by Peter Lynch and John Rothchild (Fireside, 1995) was conceived as a textbook for high school students and undergrads. However, it's one of the best primers on investing that anyone at any age can read. It will also make you laugh.

Making the Most of Your Money by Jane Bryant Quinn (Simon and Schuster, 1997). If you think you would feel better owning one big book on money, this is it. Quinn covers everything from bank accounts, credit cards, and insurance, to investing and estate planning. It's easy, general reading.

NEWSLETTERS

DO YOU NEED TO BUY A book about Roth IRAs, retirement investment strategies, or stock-picking techniques? Only if you can't find anything better to read. Stay current by reading one or two solid financial magazines each month. Consider subscribing to a financial or mutual fund newsletter—the more straightforward, the better:

The No-Load Fund Investor, edited by Sheldon Jacobs, Irvington-on-Hudson, New York, has been around longer than the rest, and it's still a solid read. Brief commentary, a model retirement portfolio, news and performance data on 1,000 funds. 800-252-2042. Monthly. $135/year.

FundsNet Insight, edited by Eric Kobren, Mutual Fund Investors Association, Wellesley, Massachusetts. Kobren's staff approaches funds and managers the same way most funds and managers approach stocks and bonds: with "fundamental research." They are thorough and smart. 800-386-3763. Monthly. $99 for new subscribers; $127 for renewals.

WEB SITES

The Individual Investor's Guide to Web Sites is a special pull-out feature in each September's issue of the American Association of Individual Investors Journal. This comprehensive list of financial and mutual fund company Web sites is a great resource. It itemizes the information you'll find at each site, notes whether it's available free or for a fee, and gives it a rating.

www.annuityshopper.com. I'm surprised this site is not on the 1998 AAII list. It's a great way to compare annuity rates, which you can also contrast with estimates of how much income you think you can generate from your own assets.

www.rothira.com. Designed for professional practitioners, this site features a wealth of information on the timely topic of the Roth IRA. It can be difficult to sort through, but it's a good way to stay on top of recent tax law changes.

www.ssa.gov. Social Security on-line. A work in progress, but you can find answers to many of your questions, as well as order forms. But you can't apply for Social Security on the Web. At least, not yet.

GLOSSARY

Adjusted Gross Income (AGI). Total taxable income.

After-tax savings. Savings on which you've already paid income tax. You can't roll over after-tax savings.

Annuitant. The person who receives annuity payments.

Annuity. A series of payments guaranteed to last until death, or over a specific time period, such as ten or twenty years. Annuity payments may be fixed or variable.

Asset allocation fund. A mutual fund that divides its assets among stocks, bonds, and cash and shifts the mix from time to time to reflect changing market conditions.

Beneficiary. The person you name to receive the benefits from your retirement plan, insurance policy, or trust after you die.

Commingle. To mix assets from a qualified plan with assets from a nonqualified plan.

Contingent beneficiary. The person you name to receive benefits from your assets after you die but only under specified circumstances, such as the death of the primary beneficiary.

Cost basis. Sometimes simply known as "basis," the amount treated as the purchase price or cost of an asset for the purpose of figuring a taxable gain or loss when it's sold.

Custodial agreement. The official document of an individual retirement savings plan, such as an IRA.

Declining balance. A method of recalculating life expectancy that subtracts one year for each year you withdraw money from your plan(s). Also called *fixed term.*

Defined benefit plan. A type of workplace retirement plan that specifies both the amount and the timing of your retirement benefit as well as a formula for calculating it.

Defined contribution plan. A type of workplace retirement plan that specifies how much an employee and/or employer can contribute, how contributions are made, and when they are made.

Distribution. A payout from your retirement plan to you or your beneficiary.

EBRI. The Employee Benefit Research Institute, a nonprofit, nonpartisan organization established in 1978 to advance the public's knowledge and understanding of employee benefits. EBRI is headquartered in Washington, D.C.

ERISA. The Employee Retirement Income Security Act of 1974.

Estate. All of your property, both physical and intellectual.

Financial supermarket. A financial company that offers a wide variety of products and services, including mutual funds, individual securities, annuities, and insurance.

Fixed term. See **Declining balance.**

Irrevocable trust. A trust that can't be changed or terminated by the person who created it.

Joint life expectancy. The number of years that two people—e.g., a husband and wife, or a husband and child named as a beneficiary—are expected to live, based on standard mortality tables.

Lump-sum distribution. According to the IRS, a distribution of the entire balance of all qualified plans of a similar type taken in one taxable year.

Net unrealized appreciation. The amount by which an asset has increased in value and on which taxes have not yet been paid.

Nonqualified plan. Strictly speaking, a retirement or savings plan that does not qualify under Section 401 of the Internal Revenue Code.

Per capita. A method of designating a beneficiary that ensures an equal division of your estate among your beneficiaries.

Per stirpes. A method of designating a beneficiary that ensures that the same portion of your estate would be passed down to and divided among the next generation of beneficiaries if one of your immediate beneficiaries died before you did.

Plan document. A required, official written description of the policies and procedures of a qualified plan.

Qualified plan. A retirement or savings plan that is qualified to receive tax benefits because it meets criteria established under Section 401 of the Internal Revenue Code.

Recalculated life expectancy. A method for redetermining life expectancy that uses an accepted formula to reduce your life expectancy by less than one year for each year you withdraw money from your plan(s).

Required beginning date. The date on which you're required to begin required minimum distributions. For most people, it's April 1 of the year after the one in which they turn 70½.

Required minimum distribution. The amount of money you're required to take from your retirement savings plans after you quit working or turn 70½, depending on the rules of the plans.

Revocable trust. A trust that can be altered or canceled by the person who created it.

Tax-deferred savings. Savings on which you've postponed the payment of taxes, typically until you withdraw them.

Term certain or period certain. A specified period of time, such as ten or twenty years, associated with the distribution of an annuity or the calculation of minimum withdrawals from a retirement plan.

Trustee. The person who holds legal title to the property in a trust, such as a retirement plan.

Vesting. The process of qualifying to receive a benefit that you may keep after separating from service or that would go to your beneficiary if you died. The vested amount of your benefit is the portion that you are eligible to receive.

Withdrawal. A distribution from a retirement savings plan that puts the money into your hands and therefore makes it taxable income in the year you receive it.

INDEX

[NOTE: Page numbers for entries occurring in boxes are suffixed with a b.]

ABOUT BLOOMBERG

Bloomberg L.P., founded in 1981, is a global information services, news, and media company. Headquartered in New York, the company has nine sales offices, two data centers, and 80 news bureaus worldwide.

Bloomberg Financial Markets, serving customers in 100 countries around the world, holds a unique position within the financial services industry by providing an unparalleled combination of news, information, and analytic tools in a single package known as the BLOOMBERG® service. Corporations, banks, money management firms, financial exchanges, insurance companies, and many other entities and organizations rely on Bloomberg as their primary source of information.

BLOOMBERG NEWS℠, founded in 1990, offers worldwide coverage of economies, companies, industries, governments, financial markets, politics, and sports. The news service is the main content provider for Bloomberg's broadcast media, which include BLOOMBERG TELEVISION®— the 24-hour cable television network available in ten languages worldwide—and BLOOMBERG NEWS RADIO™—an international radio network anchored by flagship station BLOOMBERG NEWS RADIO AM 1130℠ in New York.

In addition to the BLOOMBERG PRESS® line of books, Bloomberg publishes BLOOMBERG® MAGAZINE, BLOOMBERG PERSONAL FINANCE™, and BLOOMBERG WEALTH MANAGER™.

To learn more about Bloomberg, call a sales representative at:

Frankfurt:	49-69-920-410	San Francisco:	1-415-912-2960
Hong Kong:	852-977-6000	São Paulo:	5511-3048-4500
London:	44-171-330-7500	Singapore:	65-438-8585
New York:	1-212-318-2000	Sydney:	61-29-777-8686
Princeton:	1-609-279-3000	Tokyo:	81-3-3201-8900

ABOUT THE AUTHOR

Margaret A. Malaspina is principal of Malaspina Communications, a Massachusetts-based firm that specializes in financial communications and consulting for some of the country's largest investment firms. A former vice president at Fidelity Investments, Malaspina helped forge Fidelity's corporate communications strategies in the early 1980s. She created the firm's book publishing venture, launched the writing career of best-selling fund manager turned author Peter Lynch, and was part of the executive management team that started *Worth* magazine. She resides in Needham, Massachusetts.